Use It:

Turn Setbacks Into Success

By

Cheryl Hunter

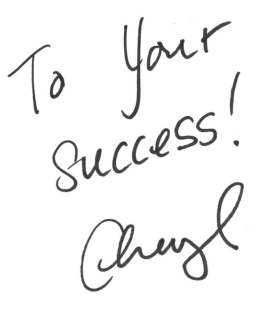

ISBN 10: 0985832401   ISBN-13: 978-0-985-83240-7

© Logos, Images courtesy of Cheryl Hunter
Cover Art: Cheryl Hunter

For more information visit: www.CherylHunter.com

9 8 7 6 5 4 3 2 1
Published in the United States of America.

Use It:

Turn Setbacks Into Success

By

Cheryl Hunter

ADVANCE PRAISE FOR USE IT

"I enjoyed reading this book. It is one powerful Chicken Soup story that contains some really great insights about what it means to be human and how to overcome the difficult experiences we inevitably experience along life's journey. It is a thoroughly engaging and quick read that will uplift your spirits and help set you free to fully enjoy this mystery we call life— no matter what."

-Jack Canfield, Co-author of the #1 New York Times
Bestselling Chicken Soup for the Soul" series

"This book is raw and real. Not only does Cheryl Hunter detail some of the most difficult, if not shattering moments of her own life, but she shows how anyone can move through their own personal traumas, emerging triumphant and transformed. This is an amazing book, and If you apply these lessons, you'll discover that your destiny is usually revealed through the scrapes and bruises you might prefer to forget, rather than the victories you will always remember."

-James F. Twyman, New York Times Bestselling Author

"Cheryl's new book *Use It: Turn Setbacks Into Success* is required reading for those who face seemingly insurmountable circumstances yet are committed to leading an extraordinary life and leaving a lasting impact on their family, friends, community and even the world. Said simply, Cheryl Hunter is a transformational rockstar!"

-Demian Lichtenstein, Author, Filmmaker

"A victorious tale about becoming the hero of your own life. Cheryl Hunter is a gifted storyteller who masterfully weaves humor into life's tragedies in a way that will make your spirit soar. Through this character's journey, we see that we are bigger than any circumstance and that our true nature is to triumph. Experience it for yourself."

-Mark Victor Hansen, Co-author of the #1 New York Times
Bestselling Chicken Soup for the Soul series

Contents

An Introduction to Alchemy

This book features my educational model the *Life Alchemy Method™*. Before we delve into the method itself, it's first essential to appreciate the namesake of the title.

Alchemy
Pronunciation: /ˈal-kə-me /
Function: noun

1. A form of chemistry and speculative philosophy practiced in medieval times whose principal aim was the transmutation of the base metals into gold.

2. The process of transmuting an every day, common substance, usually one of little or no value, into a substance of great value and worth.

The intention of the *Life Alchemy Method* is to transmute all of the "lead" in your life into "gold."

PART ONE

The Abduction

Chapter One

Werewolf

The moment it hits me—that this is going to happen no matter what I do, and that there is nothing I can do to stop it—I begin to whimper.

"Please let me go...please don't...please. I need to go home now."

He starts to make a deep guttural noise like a werewolf would in a horror movie.

In response, for some reason, I mutter things about my family; I don't know if I am losing my wits or if I am keenly thinking on my feet and getting him to relate to me as a person—in the hopes that if he sees me as another human being with a life and feelings and a family he will show me pity and release me.

"My little brother has been having problems in school," I say. "They held him back a year when he was in middle school—which they shouldn't have done—I mean; he was probably just bored because he's definitely not stupid. You should see the things he invents…"

I slow my speaking to a standstill when I notice he is growling at me really ferociously now. He turns and stares right into my eyes and slaps me hard across the face—so hard I can hear ringing in my ears afterwards.

I involuntarily start whimpering again.

"Please don't. Please. Please no. Please…"

He becomes truly like a werewolf now; he growls at full voice as he flings me across the room with his arm. I slide across the floor, and he runs at me, kicking as he comes. I become aware of the oddest thudding sound. Eventually it dawns on me: that the sound is me; I'm involuntarily letting out air each time he kicks me.

I begin whimpering again, this time to placate him and calm him down.

"Okay. Okay…okay…okay…okay…"

It works. He stops. For a moment. With one last punch across the right side of my skull to remind me who's boss, he throws himself down on top of me and stares at me with teeth bared.

Silently, without making a sound, I wet myself. I've heard the saying before, "I was so scared I peed my pants." but little did I know that the phrase was founded in reality.

He feels how wet I am—from the pee—and he thinks I am wet for him. How deluded can the guy be? Does he not smell the urine? Does he think if this sick situation gets him off that I am turned on, too? I stop trying to figure him out; this is no time for logic.

His hands feel jagged and greedy as they plunge and scrape inside of me and out. Something sharp pokes into me; could he have a knife down there or a sharp stick? I put it out of my mind. Hard and forcefully he rubs and shoves his penis back and forth over my pee-soaked crotch. Does he consider this shit foreplay?

"Your machine is so wet. Your machine wants me. Your tight little machine is begging for it. Your machine is so dirty; I am going to take it. I am going to take that dirty, wet little machine of yours."

I'm no expert on the French language, but I'm pretty sure that however in the hell "machine" translates from French, it sure ain't *vagina.*

He is on top of and inside me in no time, holding me down by planting his fist in the little soft spot on my throat. I let it go; the inability to breathe is the last of my problems. This is happening, and there is nothing I can do about it. A series of thoughts come to my mind, each in the form of fully-completed sentences and each one more condemning than the last:

"My life is ruined."

"I am no longer a good person."

"I am going to hell."

"I am disgusting and filthy and dirty now."

"I always knew something terrible was going to happen to me."

"These men are going to kill me. Good. I deserve to die now."

I need to leave my body. He is grunting wolf noises again, and I can't deal anymore, so I turn my neck as far as I can to the right and stare at the wall. There is a spot of light dancing there—it is a reflection from something outside—and it is free, whatever it is. This light is bouncing off something or other just outside, some random, lucky object that has no idea how good it has it.

I become fascinated and fixated by this little spot of light, and I stare at it with all my might and all my intention. As I stare, I feel myself morphing into it. It is gold-ish white in color, dappled with black, and as it dances with the dark, it doesn't seem afraid; it just keeps leading. The harder I stare at the spot of light, the more I feel I am a part of it, and before long I actually become it. I'm not this girl lying on a gravel-covered floor with a demonic man-wolf on top of her tearing her to shreds; I am just a shimmering spec of light that can fly away any time I choose.

Chapter Two

Playing Hooky

I grew up on a horse ranch in Rye, Colorado, a tiny town high in the Rocky Mountains, population 232. From our horse ranch, if I climb to the top of my favorite tree, I can see down into the flatlands of eastern Colorado and practically all the way to Kansas when it's clear. It's a cool contrast to be in the super-dense forests of the high mountains and to be able to see down to the dry flatlands as far as the eye can see. It feels like as close as a person can come to flying free and getting a bird's-eye view of the world.

Needless to say, Rye, Colorado, is a little different than Nice, France, but that's exactly where my journey took me.

It's not that growing up high in the Rockies miles from the closest neighbor was a rough upbringing; it was anything but. It's just that the idyllic life started wearing a little thin by the time I hit my teens; I longed to be anywhere there was civilization. One day I played hooky and concocted my master plan; I rode into town on my mini bike, picked up a *Glamour* magazine and a root beer and rushed home. With my fashion mag in hand serving as vocational advice, I plopped myself down in a meadow and began reading. I wasn't sure what I wanted to do with my life—besides getting the heck out of Rye—except I had a fervent hope that whatever life path I chose, it wouldn't require me to do math.

Glamour had an article about actresses in Hollywood; apparently the big Hollywood moviemakers were discovering actresses from modeling agencies. The article said that it was very difficult to find models that could act. The moviemakers seemed to be implying that long legs and the ability to string together two sentences is a rarity. I was on to something: I loved to read; I'm so tall that I played on the boys' basketball team throughout middle school, and according to my sister and brother: you can't get me to shut up.

This was the ticket! My mind was set; the die was cast. I had figured out my game plan! I was going to become a model and then be plucked from obscurity and made into a world-famous actress. My new game plan would not only get me out of Rye, it would eliminate forever the possibility of me having to do math—ever—for the rest of my life. Not bad work for one day of hooky!

Now I just had to get myself someplace in the world where they needed models.

Chapter Three

France

After graduating high school my best friend Lizzie and I decide to move to Europe together. We were thinking of eventually settling in London—or maybe Paris—but first we got a Eurail pass, and we began traveling around Europe for a couple of months.

We're newly into our trip, and we arrive in Nice, in southern France. It's so magical with the city meeting the glistening turquoise sea, and all the people—both men and women alike are dressed impeccably in a style that is unmistakably European.

Lizzie and I find a small *pensione* for a couple of nights then head to a sidewalk café because we're starved.

"Do you want wine?" Lizzie asks, "To celebrate?"

I almost forgot in all the travel; in two days it would be my nineteenth birthday.

Two men sauntered up and stopped at our table. They were kind of gruff and abrasive, and we were about to ask them to leave—or have the waiter do so—when one of them asked if I was a model.

My ears perked up. I said yes, living in my imagination.

The man who had asked me if I was a model had what appeared to be an expensive Kodak camera around his neck, so when he said he was a famous photographer and could make me a supermodel, I believed him without hesitation, despite the fact that Lizzie was smirking and shaking her head "no."

One of the two men was very tall and big, and he kept pushing closer and closer to our table finally pushing up against Lizzie's arm, although oddly, he never said a word and scarcely made eye contact with either of us.

Lizzie is not one to take any guff, so she asked the big man to back off and stop touching her.

The man with the camera flipped out; he snapped at Lizzie and told her she knew nothing; he said that the pinkie ring he was wearing was worth more than her father would ever make in his lifetime.

Then the man with the camera told me that if I wanted to become a model I should meet him later. He took a business card from someone and wrote a location on the back of the card and told me to meet him there.

The two men left.

Lizzie told me I was not going and that was that. She was the voice of reason; after all we had made a vow to our mothers that we would never split up no matter what. That vow was the sole condition that allowed us to make the trip.

I worried that I'd miss my big break if I didn't go meet the man with the camera and I'd never be able to fulfill my dream.

"I'm just a cowgirl from Colorado who doesn't know anybody in the modeling business," I thought to myself, "This is probably my one and only chance."

I went to meet him.

Somehow he drugged me; he gave me a glass of wine, so I suspect that's how he did it. Then he and the big man took me out of town to an abandoned construction site and left me there.

They came back at some point, and they brutally beat and raped me. While I was there I had no grasp of time, because the room in which they held me was continually dark.

All along I suspected that they'd kill me; after all, I *had* seen their faces, and they'd committed unspeakable acts to me. At one point they brought me water, which must have been drugged, too; I drifted in and out of consciousness the entire time I was there.

Three days later they dumped me in a park in Nice.

PART TWO

The Ascent

Chapter Four

Starting Over Again

As is no doubt understandable, it was a long road back.

I went through a lot of phases.

At first I pretended everything was fine.

Then I became jumpy—everything frightened me for a time—until the irritation phase set in.

After that, I began to hate everything. At first I hated dark men, or men with accents. Then I began to hate all men. I hated myself because I knew I was guilty—not "responsible" but "guilty." I hated my friends and family for not knowing and for not coming to my aid, and yet I refused to tell them…I didn't tell a soul about the abduction for nearly a decade.

My day-to-day experience became very dark, isolated and alone. I felt damaged, dirty and broken.

I was walking down the street one day in New York City and saw someone standing out on the street in Times Square with a sign saying, "Repent or go to hell!"

I thought to myself, "I'm in hell right now. No supposed, fiery depths of hell could get any worse."

In that moment it became clear I needed to start over again.

"But how do I do that?" I asked myself. "More importantly, where do I start?"

I realized that, more important than *where* I start was simply *that* I start. That being the case, it came to me that I may as well start here, where I am, and do so right now.

I took a deep breath and looked at my life.

Immediately my mind went to the abduction, and while at the time I can't say that I was yet ready to forgive them, I began comprehending a much larger view on the subject: I no longer wanted that incident to define me.

The *man with the camera* and *the big man* took my innocence and my trust and my love of life—but they did so in that very moment alone, and they did not do that forever.

My being jaded and wary and dead now was not punishing *them*; it was punishing me. They took enough from me. I decided not to let them take any more from me than they already had.

From that point forward, I put my foot down.

They do *not* get to take from me any longer!

Chapter Five

The Creation of a New Path

So great. I'd decided that I was going to move on and no longer let my past decide my present and my future. Then I was faced with the question of *how*. The decision to move on is great, and all, but how in the heck does a person actually do that? Is it sheer force of will? Is it a function of some magical Divine intervention? Did I need to move up to the Himalayas or join an ashram or give up all of my worldly goods? Should I find a guru? I didn't want to do any of that junk; I just wanted to live in peace without the images of what happened continually playing in my mind. I just wanted to experience that anything I wanted was possible again—like it seemed to be before I was abducted—and I wanted to dream big again. I just wanted to love my life and love myself. While that seemed simple enough in theory, it was far from simple in execution.

In reality when I attempted to execute my "moving on" the experience was almost as disenchanting and as disempowering as it was having been ruled by the abduction.

It was almost as if I now knew no other way to be. Can you relate? My experience was that the harder I'd try to change, the harder my mind, my circumstances and everything around me would collaborate to pull me back down to where I once had been. On many occasions I felt like giving up; I felt I should just accept my fate. I'd been abducted; I'd been traumatized by the event, and that was just my lot in life. It seemed like the aftermath was more difficult to deal with in some ways than the actual events themselves had been. Ah, good times.

And then I decided to just do something. What? I had no idea; I simply decided to do whatever presented itself and to follow whatever pathway seemed to alight in front of me. There is an old spiritual precept to which I clung, "Go through the open door." People told me about classes, courses and workshops; I took them. Someone recommended a book; I read it. A therapist was suggested; I went to her. Lather, rinse, and repeat. It was not an easy progression; I've taken a ridiculous amount of courses; I've shed buckets full of tears; I've read mountains of books; I've talked myself blue in therapy, and I've re-invented the wheel probably more times than Goodyear!

Somewhere in there it hit me: let's face it; what it is to be human is to have things happen that we wish hadn't. As much as I personally loathe the saying, there's a reason why the phrase "Shit Happens" caught on like wildfire; people can relate to it. Shit, in fact, does happen. Bad stuff happens to good people. Wish as we may that it were otherwise, that is the hard, cold truth of life. So? Now what?

In my case, I decided my personal quest to find peace could eventually become something I could give away. I would become a self-help expert, as it were, so that I had something to offer people. Turns out: that's also not so easy! While there's a lot of truly revolutionary stuff out there in the self-help, personal growth, and development world, there's a lot of stuff that's not that revolutionary at all. There's a good deal of time-sucking, flouncy, quasi-spiritual, holier than thou, "my path is better than your path," and "this way is the only way," kind of stuff saturating the marketplace.

Worse yet, the really amazing and impactful stuff often takes a really long time to either learn or to implement, or requires engaging continually to be of value. I wanted a system that was reliable, no-nonsense, effective, and most of all wasn't going to take me a lifetime to master. I wanted a spiritual, transformational path that I could take on for myself, one that honored the intelligent, striving person that I already am and took into account my commitment to succeed, despite the odds.

So I created that path—in the form of an educational model—for myself. Once I'd designed a method that was both reliable and repeatable, I decided to begin sharing it with others. I got their feedback on what worked for them—as well as what didn't work so well—and I implemented their notes. I believe now that I have created a model that works.

What I've created is not *the* path; it's *a* path. What I've created is not *the only way*; it's one way. What I've created is not meant to *replace* whatever else you've found that works; it's meant to augment whatever else you are already using that works for you. There is nothing for you to "join" and certainly nothing to conflict with the beliefs you hold; just take what works for you and discard the rest.

I trust that you're already on a path; you're already a seeker; you're already accomplished; you already know what works for you. Of course you do; you're the kind of person who would buy a book like this. I'll speak to you as the intelligent, committed person that you are.

As a seeker myself, I first studied a lot of different methods, and then I taught a lot of different methods. While each method I studied and taught absolutely has its own slant and its own take on who we are and why we do what we do, there is nothing new under the sun; the universal, fundamental truths behind everything come from common sources. If one person's packaging of those universal, fundamental truths provides an opening for you, then it fulfills its purpose. I hope my presentation of the universal, fundamental truths provides something of value for you.

To that end, over the years I've created an educational model called the *Life Alchemy Method*, based upon what I consider to be the *Five Fundamental Tenets* of turning your lead into gold.

Will it work for you? Only being here with an open mind and an open heart and authentically giving it a shot will tell. Consider what I'm saying. Take it for a test drive. See how you feel while you're doing so. Notice if it impacts your thoughts, your actions and your experience of your life. If this method makes a difference for you, use it as a lens through which to view your life newly.

It is important that you work through the tenets in the order that they were designed. They're designed to lead you through the various spaces that a person goes through to become resolved with the things that have happened in the past. Each fundamental tenet is designed to build upon the previous tenets; for that reason an understanding of the previous tenets are necessary to begin delving into the latter ones.

To support the work that you're doing here, I've also created a video training series and a live seminar that you can learn more about by visiting www.CherylHunter.com/training.

Chapter Six

Intention and Objective

Have you ever felt an inability to move beyond difficult circum-stances that have happened in your life, be it a death, a divorce, a breakup or any situation or event that you wish hadn't happened?

Chances are that's exactly why you're here.

Chances are you're looking for intervention because something is not working. You've had one or more unwanted circumstances in your life, and you're looking to move beyond the grip of them so that they no longer carry the day.

In this book you'll learn how to move beyond those difficult circumstances so that they are no longer running the show in your life and negatively impacting you in the present moment.

While everyone's difficult circumstances are not necessarily as traumatic as mine (and some are undeniably more so) there's something universal in all of the difficult circumstances that we all deal with in life.

It's that universality that we'll be working with and discussing in this book. No matter what has happened to you in your life, let's be honest: one thing we share as human beings is having circumstances happen that we wish had not.

The intention of this book is to empower you to live fully in the face of all that life hands you, which is oftentimes not what you would have chosen for yourself.

After having gone through that difficult circumstance in my own life, it took me many years on a journey to get back to "normal" again—to get back to where I had started. From that baseline level, it took me many more years' journey to create a life that I love. One of the objectives of this book is to shortcut that process and shave off ten to fifteen years' journey for you, so you don't have to spend that time moving through the difficult circumstances in your own life.

To accomplish that objective, I will share with you my own journey as well the case studies of other people that I have worked with using the *Life Alchemy Method*. The case studies will provide a road map for you; they will display what it looks like both to apply and not apply the *Five Fundamental Tenets* in your journey on this path and your road to victory over the difficulties you've previously faced.

Chapter Seven

The Self You Left Behind

O nce I began my road to recovery one of the most difficult issues I faced was that I felt like I was operating at reduced power. It was as if I didn't have all of myself with me anymore... if that makes any sense.

What was initially just a vague feeling that I couldn't quite articulate eventually became a substantial cornerstone of the entire *Life Alchemy Method* as I started working with others who had suffered difficult circumstances and felt a similar after-effect.

Therefore, one of the most critical items we'll address is the notion of reclaiming the "you" you've lost in the process. That happens in the first place because with each of the life-changing difficult circumstances that we face, we leave a piece of ourselves behind.

Have you ever heard someone say, "I'm going off to find myself," or "I feel like I've lost myself," or, "I don't know who I am anymore"? Have you ever *been* the person saying things like that? There's a reason why those are common phrases the world over: because we really do lose a bit of ourselves at each one of those incomplete incidents. When we leave a piece of ourselves behind, we may end up belaboring the fact, obsessing over it, or even acting differently in the present because of it. One thing is certain: we're not firing on all cylinders.

Imagine, if you will, that a person is a knit-together being, and at each one of these incidents some part of the person gets snagged and held onto, so that as the person moves forward through time, less and less of their self moves forward with that person. It's as if, when that difficult incident got a hold of us, we've continued to unravel forward into present day until we're like a threadbare pile of yarn.

One of the primary intentions of this book is that, as you complete each of the difficult incidents from your past, you will reclaim those parts of yourself that you left behind. Once you reclaim the parts of yourself that you left behind, you will have your full capacities, abilities, and faculties available to you. Your world will open up.

As you work with each of the *Five Fundamental Tenets*, you will be left with more of yourself, and you will be left with power not only over those past circumstances, but also over any difficult circumstances that may arise in the future. You'll be left with the ability to simply enjoy your life. Feelings of resentment, and regret, and longing for life to be different, will start to clear up of their own accord.

Chapter Eight

Use It

I was on a path and I started to feel some relief. While I was in no way happy or healed yet, the light was showing up at the end of the tunnel so to speak. I had not yet really delved into the abduction much; truth be told, I was mostly skirting the issue. I was getting enough relief in the process though, that I started to get bought off by that relief.

Have you ever noticed that for yourself or by watching others? It's like swinging on a polarity somewhere between abject horror and absolute bliss, and once we start edging out of abject horror enough to feel relief we get bought off and become content. It's like, "Whew! The hideousness is over! I can take it easy now!"

Problem is if we never keep the upward momentum going we'll slide back into abject horror before long. There is no staying still in life; we're either moving forward or we're moving back—period. Don't believe me? Try standing still as the world passes you by. See what happens? As they move forward, you, by virtue of not moving, are effectively moving backwards!

So there I was, getting bought off by the momentary experience of relief when I had a cockeyed plan: I was just going to not deal with the abduction; I was going to continue to push it down and *never* deal with it. After all, I was feeling better now that my life was not complete hell, right?

Thank God the Universe smacked me on the behind.

I was out to dinner with my boyfriend (and his parents whom I loved dearly) at the time. His father was one of those salty, dry New Yorkers; he had the greatest sense of humor ever. Sure, my boyfriend's father was often inappropriate with his jokes; but the fact that he said things to get a rise out of people only made me adore him more.

We were at a totally ritzy restaurant on the Upper East Side and we were all dressed to the nines. Someone at the next table was talking so loudly that we overheard his conversation; it seemed the feds were coming to shut down his company. Apparently, the man said, the feds were going to sell off all of the assets piece-by-piece and leave the company without a penny to its name.

My boyfriend's father said, "If rape is inevitable, you may as well lie back and enjoy it."

Some people were aghast; others laughed. Normally I would have laughed; this time his joke was too close to home. Mind you; he didn't have any idea I'd ever been raped; I'd never breathed a word to a soul. Typically I loved the way he rubbed people the wrong way; this was not one of those times.

That night I lie awake all night, vacillating between fury and grief. I was too upset to sleep, and all over a little one-sentence joke. I realized that if some innocuous thing like that could make me lose it, I was out of my mind thinking I could somehow live a great life while shoving my past under the rug.

I was going to have to *use it*.

There was no way out but through; there was no getting around this one. The only way I'd ever be free would be if I'd go straight through the center of my demon.

As much as you may hate to hear it, that's where I'm taking you, dear reader, as well.

For that reason the next objective of the book is to empower you to actually *use it*. Use *what?* To use all that life has handed you—including the difficult circumstances that you wish life had *not* handed you—to live the life of your dreams.

The point is not that you trudge through those difficult circumstances, events, and occurrences in life; the point is not about working around them; the point is definitely not about tolerating them. You have *trudged through, worked around and tolerated enough for one lifetime!* The point is that you *use* those exact circumstances, events and occurrences as the access to the life about which you dream!

If you think that sounds like a stretch, an impossibility or a fantasy, you're not alone. That is what you will learn how to do over the course of this book.

First though, here's a little bit about where the notion of "using it" arose.

Although many people might say the term "use it," to mean different things, I first learned the term from the acting business (I was an actress for many years).

I was in New York City, when my acting teacher brought it up. She said something like this: "As an actor your instrument is you—your body, your voice, your thoughts, your mind, your emotions, your feelings and your life. You are your only instrument, so if there's something in your space, your life, your circumstances or your world, there's no way around it. You can pretend it's not there, but pretending that will make you detached and not present. Anything other than 'using' what's already there for you leads to cruddy acting. It also leads to a distanced experience for the audience and an inauthentic experience for the actor, which then, of course, causes the distanced experience for the audience. Again, that leads to cruddy acting."

Shortly after that I had what was to be the biggest audition of any kind I had ever gone up for; it was for a series regular in a new TV show. I had been called back to audition repeatedly. Each time I worked with my coach beforehand. This time I was meeting with the network and studio executives.

As fate would have it, my boyfriend at the time (the one with the funny father) broke up with me that very day after three long days of fighting. I brushed off the breakup, and I went to the audition as if everything were fine, forgetting completely about 'using it.'

I desperately wanted something other in my space than what was there, which was, "I've just been dumped, and I think I'm going to die." The role called for me to be this happy young girl who had just gotten the job of a lifetime. That was pretty much an impossible prospect; I was just pretending to be happy go-lucky on top of, "Oh God, my life is over." Needless to say I bombed the audition. I was like a zombie; I was neither happy nor sad. A wooden cutout of me could have played the role better.

When I got home later on that evening, I debriefed the audition over the phone with my coach. I burst into tears and told her my boyfriend and I broke up that day. She sweetly asked, "Did you use it in your audition?" I was so confused I didn't know what she meant. I asked her how I could have possibly "used it" because the emotions were so vastly different; there's quite a disparity between feeling like my life is ending because my love dumped me and feeling elated because I just got a great job. I could hear her smile through the phone as she spoke.

"All you have is what's already there, given your only 'instrument' is you: your emotions, your body, your feelings, your expression, your words. If some emotion, some event or some circumstance happens in your life that you are dealing with—good or bad—the only thing that you can do is to use it. There is no way around the thing, there is no pretending it isn't there, there is only to use what is already there and happening."

My acting teacher explained that whatever emotion I'm feeling at any particular moment may be inappropriate to the context of the scene but, she said, "If you allow the emotion that is there to just "be," it will let you be. What you resist persists," she added, "So if you resist heartbreak, the heartbreak will have you by the throat."

"So you mean..." I asked, "If I've just broken up with some-one...and I'm supposed to be a happy, carefree, joyous girl, then I have to go *through the heart of the sadness and despair* and just say the words?"

"What's your alternative?" She asked.

"Deny that the sadness and despair is there and be the robot I was this afternoon?" I laughed, smiling for the first time in three days.

"Bingo," she said warmly. "There's no way around...only through. The "right emotion" will sort itself out; just allow what's there to be."

I didn't get the job, obviously, but I left with a far more valuable lesson. Applied to the whole of life, the lesson of *use it* is a profound one.

I became certain we'd have to use the exact circumstances in our lives that have been troubling us and shutting off our access to joy and satisfaction to live the lives of our dreams.

PART THREE

The Method

TENET NUMBER ONE:

Your Thoughts Are Not Your Friends™

Chapter Nine

Tenet Number One:

Your Thoughts Are Not Your Friends

"The highest possible stage in moral culture is when we recognize that we ought to control our thoughts."

-Charles Darwin

So here I was, struggling to get back to "normal" again, whatever that was, and I was engaged in an intense learning period. As I studied, something became evident very quickly: other people were dealing with similar roadblocks, hurdles and challenges like I was. Whether they were people in seminars with me, people writing the books that I read, or those who were used as examples and case studies in what I was learning, it seemed like all people were up against a common set of phenomena. It didn't mean we'd all experienced the same things or that we'd shared a past or that we'd gone through the same circumstances. We all were from varied walks of life with totally different histories. What we did share was a similar road to travel when attempting to live a fulfilled life.

That's when it hit me: the journey I was taking was not a personal journey; it was a journey common to human beings.

For that reason, the "conversation" of this book will not be a personal conversation; the topics, distinctions and ideas we address will not be personal ones; this subject matter isn't really about *personal* phenomena.

Don't get me wrong; we'll address things along this journey that will be deeply personal to you. In fact the philosophies in this book are actually designed to bring up an experience and a world that is *uniquely* yours, but it's important to remember that we're addressing phenomena that are common to human beings, they are things which all people share.

The topics we'll be addressing throughout this book will be the same; they are phenomena related to the design of human beings.

Putting the *Life Alchemy Method* to work in your life will require something of you; the method may be difficult to get through, and facing the parts of your life that you've not dealt with in this way may be confronting. If you can relate to what is being distinguished and presented as human phenomena, rather than as a personal indictment or as an indication of any imagined personal shortcomings, then you'll have the objectivity needed to complete the exercises in this book in such a way that can make a real and lasting difference in your life.

For me, knowing that *everyone* deals with this stuff gave me the breathing room to address my life head on. At least I knew I was in good company!

There's a term that I want to make clear while I'm on the subject of common human phenomena. I'm going to be using the term *"humanness"* to encapsulate everything built in to your human make-up. The actual definition will shed some light on what I'm pointing to, here.

Human·ness

Pronunciation: / ˈhyoo-mən-nəss/

Function: adjective

1. Of, relating to, or characteristic of humans.
2. Having or showing positive aspects of nature and character.
3. Subject to or indicative of weaknesses, imperfections, and fragility.

It's worth noting that while the term *humanness* signifies the positive aspects of being a human, it also includes the "down-side" of being human as well, and the weaknesses, imperfections and fragility that we all embody to a greater or lesser degree.

If we were talking about cars, we could say that your "humanness" is everything that comes factory standard. When I use that term it's meant to include your subconscious, your unconscious, your instincts, your inner child, your self-preservation reflexes, your persona, your thoughts, the repetitive conversations you have with yourself, etc. It is a deliberately broad description to represent anything that's automatically there and that is not characterized by conscious, generated thought, action, and ways of being.

So here I was on the road to recovery and I had made a massive discovery: all of the things I was struggling with were not unique to me; they were built-in and common to all people. That gave me enough objectivity to plan the next step. I felt terrible all the time; I had never breathed a word of the abduction to anyone, and I was in dire need of getting out of my own head. Without saying why, I told my mom I was depressed. She'd never dealt with depression, so she wasn't sure where to point me. She said, "Find some people who are worse off than you are, and help them."

It sounded like as good a plan as any.

I pondered, "I'm young, depressed, and screwed in the head. Who is worse off than I am?" The answer came to me, "People who are *old*, depressed and screwed in the head!"

I decided that old-age homes were my answer: I would volunteer there. I dug old people; my grandma was my favorite person in the world, so I knew we'd get along just fine. Best of all, it would get me out of my head. Hopefully, it would get them out of their heads, too.

What started out as a temporary fix ended up being a long-term arrangement. For over a decade, I volunteered extensively with elderly people in various end stages of life—from assisted-living facilities to nursing homes to Alzheimer's and dementia-care facilities.

All of the people with whom I volunteered had some degree of dementia or Alzheimer's. The thing about that commonality is that those people's persistent thoughts are generally shared out loud. In spending time with those individuals, I noticed that they always seemed to be "caught in a loop" of repetitive patterns of thought and/or conversations.

The woman with whom I was closest was Rose, and she was an assistant costumer for movies back in the "Golden Era of Hollywood." Rose had constant themes in her conversation that revolved around rushing around at work, and a constant, recurring cast of characters: Frank, Travis, and Rita, in particular.

A typical day might involve me going over to the nursing home where Rose lived. She'd typically be in one of the communal rooms but almost never anywhere that a television was playing. I'd look for her across the room for a moment, and from the moment we saw each other, it would begin.

"Rita's not happy with the dresses. And if Rita's not happy, nobody is happy. I need you to get the fit model back in here on the double, see? And make it snappy."

In the very beginning I made more than a few attempts to reason with her: Rita wasn't here now, and we weren't at the studio; we were at her new home. Finally I caved in and just started playing along. It didn't hurt anyone to play along, and it sure did make Rose a happy camper.

"I've just come from seeing Rita, and she's thrilled with the dresses!" I'd say, walking in the nursing home, watching the relief wash over Rose's face. Before long, however, it would start again.

"Rita's not happy with the dresses...looks like we're going to have to pull an all-nighter until we can get them right. If Rita is not happy, Travis will be on the warpath. And if Travis is on the warpath, you know what that means?"

Not surprisingly, I did. We'd been through this imaginary scenario hundreds of times. "It means Frank will be on the warpath, too."

"Ain't it the truth?" Rose would respond, shaking her head.

Some time later, once I'd figured out how the conversations were going to go with Rose, I'd try to be proactive about it; I'd enter the nursing home ready to launch in about how I'd just run into Travis and Frank and Rita all together at once and everybody loved the dresses. Despite my efforts, the same concerns would re-surface and Rose would be back to worrying about Rita and the dresses again. More often than not her concerns would surface mere seconds after I had just addressed them; it seemed all but impossible to make them go away.

I started calling those persistent, repetitive thoughts and conversations "thought loops," because of the nature of the way they do just that; they loop around and repeat virtually verbatim as if they're on a track.

When I first started spending time with Rose and the others, I found that those thought loops were unbearable; the person's conversation was always and forever about the same thing. I actually contemplated moving on entirely and finding a new way to contribute my time and get out of my head rather than volunteering with elderly people.

"These people and their thought loops are driving me nuts!" I'd tell myself.

Suddenly I realized why they were driving me so nutty: because I do the same exact thing!

I saw that my thoughts and conversations looped in the same way about things I would have or could have or should have done but didn't. My thoughts and conversations looped about what the people who abducted me needed to be told and what unspeakable acts should be done to them in return. My thoughts and conversations looped about what my friends and family should have done since the abduction but didn't. My thoughts and conversations looped about why I couldn't tell my friends and family what had happened in the first place.

I, like Rose, had constant themes in my thoughts/conversations—they generally revolved around having been abducted—and I too had a constant, recurring cast of characters. The only difference between Rose and me was that my thought loops were not said aloud—usually. And my stories didn't contain a Frank, Travis, or Rita, and there were definitely no dresses. Other than that, Rose and I were the same.

Don't misunderstand me; I'm not attempting to draw a correlation between having thought loops and having Alzheimer's-related dementia or dementia in general. Rather, I'm suggesting that because Rose and the others with whom I volunteered did have some form of dementia, each of them spoke their internal dialogue aloud, which gave me the rare opportunity to be able to take a peek inside of their mind, as it were. Typically our internal dialogues are just that—they're internal—so no one really knows what goes on inside of the mind of another.

The fact that Rose and the others "thought aloud" enabled me to witness the pervasive nature of the well-worn neural pathways as thought loops that get formed when a person persistently thinks about unresolved or troubling issues in their lives. Rose and the others became a cautionary tale about the importance of resolving the impact of our unwanted circumstances, and the necessity of consciously directing our minds to form neural pathways that we are committed to, rather than being subject to those which happen by default.

I was getting really excited by what I was learning. Between my own personal-development study, coupled with the immense experience I was getting by spending time with the elderly people and witnessing their thought loops, I became certain of three things:

1. Those crazy-making, maddening, persistent thought loops are a common human phenomena, not my own private hell.

2. I should not believe everything I think.

3. My thoughts are not my friends.

With that newfound revelation I decided to dive in further by distinguishing what was at play in my own thought loops, and then researching as much as I could on the brain and the way we think.

One of the things I discovered that was at the heart of my thought loops and suffering was what I began calling the "one-two punch." I saw that there's a "one-two punch" aspect of what happens when we suffer from unwanted circumstances. First, the unwanted circumstance itself happens. That brings up all manner of negative emotion. Then we engage in incessant, harsh self-talk about the incident, which elicits even more negative emotion.

The problem quickly becomes the fact that we have not only primary emotions but also secondary ones; we compound emotion without realizing we are doing so.

When the unwanted circumstance happens, we feel correlate emotion: stress, anger, resentment, or sadness, for example; then we feel a secondary emotion in response to the initial emotion, such as, "I am furious that I've been sad and resentful for so long!" Hence the phrase "one-two punch."

This means we suffer twice; first we suffer from the unwanted circumstance itself, then from the fallout of the unwanted circumstance.

Another problem is that the "fallout" is not a one-time affair; we have thoughts about the unwanted circumstance, and before long the thoughts become obsessive. Why? Because repetitive thought literally alters our brain. You may have heard the phrase, "neurons that fire together wire together." What happens when we have repeated thought or take repeated action is that the neurons in our brain wire together and groove neural pathways as shortcuts between the neurons involved.

Once those neural pathways become well worn, the thoughts we've been repeatedly thinking become habitual and non-ending, and it becomes increasingly different to think anything new.

Most of the thoughts that we are thinking are self-talk or *"internal dialogue,"* to use the phrase coined by Gestalt therapy in the 1940's and 1950's. There is a very specific nature to internal dialogue: it's condemning, judgmental and negative. Typically the internal dialogue is not only all of that, but it's also self-directed.

So if you consider that the modus operandi of the internal dialogue is to criticize, and the primary target of its criticism is ourselves, and then you consider that the nature of thought regarding any unresolved incident is to repeat itself, you find yourself in quite a pickle. Those negative, criticizing, endless thoughts are getting deeper and deeper ingrained into your brain and before long you become wired to think nothing else.

Can you relate? Is this providing any relief in terms of the incessant thought loops you deal with? I hope so. Don't get bought off by relief, though; keep reading. There's more to the puzzle.

1. As our brain is developing as infants and children, we are developing language simultaneously. The phenomenon of *"brain development/language development"* becomes inexorably linked.

2. As we turn that language inward, we begin to create "thought."

3. We use that developing language not only to engage in dialogue with others but also to engage in "inner dialogue" with ourselves.

Before long, we begin to start to identify ourselves with our language in a very real way. After all, language is the way that we express who and what we are, and language is the way that we process who and what we consider ourselves to be.

Ultimately, our very definition of who we are becomes enmeshed with and equivalent to our thoughts and the process of thinking. We become so enmeshed with our thoughts and our process of thinking that there is no separation in our experience between ourselves, our thought processes, and the thoughts we think. We are one in the same. That sure gives the phrase, "I think; therefore, I am," a whole new slant!

We begin to put an immense credence in our thoughts; to doubt them (if they are in fact who we are) would be akin to ceasing to exist. We become fierce believers in and defenders of our thoughts, our judgments and our opinions as right, correct, and the only way to view things.

I dug deeper to ensure that I was on to something and that these notions of thought and language and the prison of thought loops were substantiated by science. When I found the groundbreaking Dr. Michael Gazzaniga, I learned those notions are, in fact, very real.

By working with people who had a corpus callosum split, Dr. Gazzaniga spent extensive time studying the two halves of the brain. Through his study, he discovered an interesting process that occurs in the left hemisphere of the brain that he named "the Interpreter." Gazzaniga theorized that this part of the brain makes up stories about patterns that it observes.

> *"The left hemisphere makes strange input logical; it includes a special region that interprets the inputs we receive every moment and weaves them into stories to form the ongoing narrative of our self-image and our beliefs. I have called this area of the left hemisphere 'the Interpreter' because it seeks explanations for internal and external events and expands on the actual facts we experience to make sense of, or interpret: the events of our life."*

In contrast, the right half of the brain would just state the information that it knows and only that, but the left brain tries to make sense of the information and will fill in the blanks. Dr. Gazzaniga said that the left brain is creating a protagonist or "self" where we develop a unique system of beliefs. Through "the Interpreter" comes the ideas that we feel we would fight or die for. From a scientific standpoint, it is through the process of "the Interpreter" that we actually become our ideas, our thoughts, what we know, and what we believe.

Couple this with the fact that we are eternally deepening the neural pathways that we've created through this repetitive thought and you can start to comprehend upon how slippery a slope we've come.

TENET NUMBER TWO:

You Are Designed To Survive, Not Thrive ™

Chapter Ten

Tenet Number Two:

You Are Designed To Survive, Not Thrive

"The ultimate value of life depends upon awareness and the power of contemplation rather than upon mere survival."

-Aristotle

By this point I'd realized that my thoughts were not my friends, that I should not believe everything I think, and that I needed to radically change what I was thinking, how I was feeling and what I'd been doing or I was doomed to experience more of the same. The problem was twofold: first, I felt like I'd lost my mojo in life. At one point I knew I had it; now it was definitely gone, and second, I found it incredibly difficult to change.

That revelation brought me to this second tenet and the discovery of two essential landmarks on my journey: *Defining Incidents* and the fact that our survival instincts rule us completely, but we're virtually unaware of that fact.

I'll begin with *Defining Incidents* and share what those have to do with us losing our mojo.

The way a *Defining Incident* is identified is that it has these two parts:

- One: it is any incident which happens to a person and has them alter the way they view themselves and their lives, and,

- Two; there is something that person needed but failed to receive in the time period immediately surrounding that incident.

The first one is self-explanatory, so I will move to the next (what a person needed but failed to receive in the time period immediately surrounding the incident). It is the combination of the incident itself plus the unmet need and it takes what happened and turns it from being simply an *incident* to being a *Defining Incident*. Try it this way: if a person has their needs fulfilled in the time period immediately surrounding the incident, it would not compound into a *Defining Incident*; it would simply exist for that person as just another incident that happened in the course of their lifetime.

If, as an example, little Bobby was just bullied for the first time at school, and little Bobby's parents came to pick him up from school and intervened in ways that little Bobby needed them to, the incident itself could easily fade into the background after a time. If little Bobby's mother took him home and nurtured him and listened to him and held him and if his father raised holy hell with the school and the other kids' parents, and if that satisfied little Bobby, then their providing what he needed at that time could have kept the incident from compounding. If, by contrast, however, little Bobby came home from school and his mother scolded him for dirtying his clothes and his big brother made fun of him for getting picked on and then little Bobby mouthed off to his mother, which made his father beat him again when he came home, one can easily see how that could compound the incident for little Bobby into one that became a *Defining Incident*.

The nature of a *Defining Incident* is reflexive of its title; it truly does define life for the person who experiences it.

When those *Defining Incidents* happen in life, we have an immense reactive response and we begin constructing life anew in order to cope. From that point forward, life becomes one coping mechanism after the other.

At the time of your *Defining Incidents*, you construct the following:

1. Who you are,

2. How the world is, and what your place is in that world,

3. Who other people are (and *how* other people are), and,

4. How life is going to go from here on out.

As that's happening, you don't see that your creation of the "who you are," and "how the world is," and "what your place is in that world," etc. is simply a function of dragging the *Defining Incidents* along with you. The moment that you create those confining definitions, you become imprisoned by them. From that point forward, it's as if those *Defining Incidents* keep happening over and over rather than having just happened once in the past; in fact, they define the present.

To clarify: this construction of "who you are," and "how the world is," and "what your place is in that world," etc. is not a freely created, happy-go-lucky, the-world-is-my-oyster type of creation. On the contrary, what you're doing is taking a good, hard look at the *Defining Incident* that just happened, and, in an effort to prevent that from ever happening again, constructing the closest approximation you can come to at the time to whatever you think will keep you safe in the future.

The problem is this: that *Defining Incident* that just happened was a one-time deal.

Follow me here. Even if it becomes a chronic and ongoing problem like a spouse who abused you once and then goes on to do that in the future, the initial instance of abuse was a specific, one-time deal on that particular day. A person could choose to react to that *Defining Incident* in any number of ways. More often than not, each of us responds by creating some "fail-safe" mechanism to protect ourselves in the future from that very same *Defining Incident* from ever happening again. The problem is that exact same *Defining Incident* can never happen again anyway, but there's no rational logic employed in the process of creating a coping mechanism.

So now you've constructed a new post-incident version of who you are, how the world is, and what your place is in that world, etc. Problem is, that newly-constructed view has a fatal flaw: in order to operate inside of the new world that you've constructed, you have to keep dragging around the past *Defining Incident* with you everywhere you go in order to make the world you've constructed valid. A coping mechanism, by design, is reflexive of something. A coping mechanism doesn't arise on its own; it's a reaction-based piece of machinery. Reflexive of what, and reactive to what? The dadgum, horrible *Defining Incident*, that's what!

The reactive-based coping mechanism thinks it'll avoid ever having to deal with the same *Defining Incident* ever again, so it constructs a system designed to be everything that the *Defining Incident* was not. But, do you know what happens when you try too hard to be "not something"? You get that thing that you're trying "not" to be. It's reflexive of the thing itself. You can't have "not something" without having the "something" present in every moment you're trying to be "not that". That's the design flaw.

A person can have an unlimited number of *Defining Incidents*, theoretically speaking, although generally the ones that happen later in life are typically based in large part upon the earlier *Defining Incidents*.

At any point in life, we have a certain set of competencies, abilities and faculties available to us. At the time that your *Defining Incident* occurred, you were younger than you are now, and you had the competencies, abilities and faculties of a person at that age. I believe that one impact of a *Defining Incident* is that we become developmentally stuck at the age we were during our *Defining Incident*. While this doesn't mean we don't become functioning adults—we do, of course—there are areas of influence in our lives that are impacted by our being stuck, developmentally speaking.

In my case it was being stuck in the areas of dealing with men (in all contexts), sex, and romantic relationships, I was developmentally stuck back at age nineteen. I was not operating as a fully-grown woman in those areas until I was able to "grow myself up" in those arenas by getting to work on this tenet.

My fundamental assertion, and the reason I work with *Defining Incidents* in the first place is this: In life, there are two distinct states: the first state of life is the time when the world is your oyster, and the second state of life is the time when the world is not your oyster. The line of demarcation is the original *Defining Incident*. With each ensuing *Defining Incident*, the world becomes less and less "our oyster."

Another way of saying this is that there's a time when your "reality" is that you can do, or have, or be anything. You've got mojo. Later, in contrast, that is not your reality. You no longer "own the world," vis-à-vis your ability to do, have or be anything.

The real question then becomes why.

Well, first, I want you to consider a radical concept: the fact that the world is now no longer your oyster is not a bad thing, and it's not even a personal thing. There's nothing you could have done differently to have that not be the case; it's one of those things that happens to everyone, like aging or needing to eat, or reliance upon sleep to function. It's built into the human experience.

If you can take a step back from the circumstances and events that have happened in your life and see them objectively, you'll have the power to re-contextualize them and give yourself power over them.

So that addressed the mojo issue and why I felt I lost it. Now to address the reason why it seemed impossible to enact any real or lasting change in my life. Here's what I found.

Have you ever noticed that when you try to start something new or change a habit it can be incredibly difficult? Bring to mind any of your past New Year's resolutions if you doubt what I'm saying. The reason for this is that your humanness is deeply invested in homeostasis; it does not want you to change under any circumstance. Your humanness is certain the only way you'll survive is by remaining exactly the way you are right now. If you're broke, then broke works; it keeps you alive. You're unhappy, you say? Well, then your humanness's mandate is to keep you that way. Whatever way you are is the way you must stay.

The one and only job of your humanness is to secure your survival. We are hardwired to do nothing else and to automatically challenge anything that our humanness perceives as a threat to our survival.

The problem is that our humanness thinks all kinds of things are a threat to our survival that in fact are not.

We're just cruising along in life, minding our business; we think that whatever plans we think up or concoct we'll be able to fulfill just because we want to. We don't realize that by trying to do anything new, we're working against our human design that wants for us to do nothing more than stay small, stay safe, stay close to the protection of home, and stay alive.

You wonder why your life looks pretty much the same now as it did five, ten, or twenty years ago?

- Because the fundamental way we survive is we stay safe.
- The fundamental way we stay safe is we stay the same.
- Stasis equals safety.

Mystery solved: our lives never really change because we are hardwired to stay the same.

If you can acknowledge and appreciate your humanness for getting its job done—after all, here you are; you're still alive—then you can stop fighting with it. Better yet, you can partner with it and enact the changes that you want to implement *together*.

Let's face it; life can be a dangerous prospect. People die every second of every minute of every day. Your humanness knows this; its job is to ensure you survive at all costs. Contrary to your own desires and wishes to thrive, your humanness is bigger; your humanness is stronger, and your humanness will win unless you know how to work in concert with it. Its job is to ensure you survive, period.

How does your humanness accomplish that task? It devises, uses and relies upon survival mechanisms. I made a list of all of them that I was experiencing so that I could get present to the immensity of them. In order to bring a little levity to the subject, I kept in mind this quote from the writer and humorist Jane Wagner, "The ability to delude yourself may be an important survival tool."

Here is a list of the survival mechanisms I came up with:

- Learn from past mistakes.
- Try to avoid and/or prevent whatever happened in the past from happening again.
- Avoid being present. Either look back at the past or look forward into the future.
- Try to anticipate what will go wrong or could go wrong in the future.
- Don't trust people.
- Be fearful.
- Be cautious.
- Don't give yourself fully.
- Play it safe.
- Do not ever risk.
- Do only what you know works.
- Stay the same.
- Develop habits…generally bad habits.
- Tolerate an immense amount of un-workability, dissatisfaction and upset, all so you don't have to change.

- Hide the truth.

- Lie.

- Pretend.

- Cheat.

- Betray others.

- Betray yourself and your ideals.

- Try to make other people like you, accept you, and at least not be your enemy.

- Become a know-it-all.

- Get upset with, don't like, or even hate those who "do it wrong."

- If you're a country or a religion, you wage wars against, fight, and kill those who "do it wrong."

- Never hope for too much.

- Kill off your dreams.

- Kill off the hopes and dreams of those close to you.

- Control, dominate, and manipulate people, things, and circumstances.

- Choose a point-of-view (such as optimism, pessimism, being a skeptic or being spiritual) and become a champion for that point-of-view. Everything in your life shows up as a match for your chosen point-of-view. Insist that it's "just the way life is."

- On top of everything else, stay in denial.

Exhausting as it may be to read, this is by no means an exhaustive list! You may certainly find more mechanisms that you rely upon to survive. Look for yourself to discern what your own mechanisms are; distinguishing them will provide you access to seeing them as they're occurring, which will be very helpful for you as you move forward. Your access to discerning if an action or a way of being is a "survival mechanism" is that it is habitual, automatic, and crushes aliveness and vitality.

One of the chief survival mechanisms that we all share by virtue of being human is the proclivity to drag around our past with us. It's as if our humanness believes that our past is somehow the roadmap to the future, and without it we'd be lost. Bring to mind the vision of a hobo. I know; that's a politically incorrect, old-fashioned name for someone living on the streets; just roll with me for a moment. A hobo would put all of his worldly goods in a bandana tied to a stick propped over his shoulder. He'd carry that little satchel with him everywhere he went.

Unfortunately, to make the image correct, you need to picture both a hobo with a satchel along with an episode of *Hoarders: Buried Alive*. Why? Because we don't carry around *a little bit* of stuff with us, and the stuff we carry is useless junk. As human beings we carry around *everything* from the past: every insult, every slight, every hurt, every wound; we carry around every time we embarrassed ourselves, every time we felt betrayed, every time we came up short. We want to ensure that those things never, ever happen again, so we carry more and more of our past with us just in case anything remotely resembling the past should appear in the present. The problem with that method of operating is that everything in the present occurs just like the past. Every situation, every person—even ourselves—seems in some way just like the past. Which is all the more validation for taking those things that happen each and every day and rolling them up in our little bandana, tying them on our stick and tossing them over our shoulder. Except this "little satchel" couldn't fit over anyone's shoulder; you'd be lucky if you could lift that puppy using a forklift!

There's a reason why the ancients had a myth about Sisyphus; it's because it's a common human phenomenon. Every day at sunrise, Sisyphus rose with the sun, ready for a new day. He'd spend the entire day toiling to push a big boulder up the hill. It would try him; every day he'd be tested, and every day it would take everything Sisyphus had to push that immense boulder up the hill. Inevitably, at the end of each day, the immense boulder would roll down the hill, negating all the effort and work that Sisyphus had accomplished that day. The next morning the process would begin again, on and on, day after day, throughout eternity.

Here's a little something to consider: human beings are like dung beetles. If you're an easily offended person, you may want to

- Stop reading at this point,

- Get over yourself,

- Try the analogy on for size anyway, and see if you can draw any parallels in your own life.

Do you know what a dung beetle is? Go online and check out a video of them if not. Dung beetles are beetles that feed exclusively on feces. They not only feed exclusively on feces—let's go ahead and call it "dung," shall we?—the dung is the very centerpiece of their lives. They seek the dung out; they find it; they fight over it; they form it into balls; they push it around; they bury it; they lay their eggs in it, and they feed their young with it. Heck, the male dung beetle even uses dung to court and woo the female.

Essentially there are three types of dung beetles: there are rollers, who are expert at rolling dung into great big balls; there are tunnelers, who bury the dung balls, and there are dwellers, who neither roll nor bury: they simply move into the dung balls, set up camp, and call it home. There's one thing all of the dung beetles have in common, though: they all love themselves some poop.

Most dung beetles search for dung using their especially keen and sensitive sense of smell. Some dung beetles fly up to 10 miles in search of the perfect patch of dung; these are beetles on a mission. Other species simply attach themselves to larger animals and patiently await their prize.

Once a fresh pile of dung arrives on the scene, the male traditionally takes the opportunity to court a female. To do so he will offer her a giant brood ball of dung in lieu of a ring. If the female likes the male and chooses to accept his advances, the pair will scurry away together, either with both of them rolling the ball together or with the female hitchhiking atop it.

The lovebirds rush to find the perfect location to set up their abode. Once found, they mate, bury the brood ball, and lay the eggs in the dung. In approximately a week, the babies hatch, feast on the dung, and crawl back up to the surface. Then the cycle begins again, and the hunt for dung is on. They must find new dung immediately; without it they will die.

The moral of the story: *don't be a dung beetle—let your shit go!*

TENET NUMBER THREE:

You Are Responsible For Everything That

Happens In Your Life. Everything. ™

Chapter Eleven

Tenet Number Three:

You Are Responsible For Everything That Happens In Your Life. Everything.

"The truth will set you free, but first it will piss you off."
                                                    Gloria Steinem

When someone first suggested some version of this third tenet to me early on my journey, I was incensed. "How dare you!" I said to myself rather than aloud, "You obviously are an idiot who has *no goddamned idea* what I've been through!" I discounted that person and their stupid suggestion and moved on.

Before long something similar came up again when I was in a seminar. The man leading the course asked me what part I played in the horrible things that had happened in my life. I'd hinted at the fact that I'd endured a horrible situation, but I'd never said outright what had happened. Again, I was incensed; this time I was also outraged, so I responded out loud. "Are you kidding me? I was *a child!* You tell me what responsibility I could possibly have had in some random act of violence executed against me!" I couldn't believe the insensitivity and gall of the seminar leader. "This!" I thought, "From a person who pretends to be so evolved!"

The sneer on my face must have given my disdain away; the leader responded to me as if he read my inner thoughts. "I see," he said, "So you're saying that you're a victim of your circumstances and that your circumstances are in charge of your life being the way it is."

Asshole. When he put it like that *I* sounded like the idiot. I crossed my arms and sat there for the rest of the evening, but I never went back to the seminar again. His words kept me up at night, though. Literally I could not sleep as what he said rolled around in my brain. Was I a victim? Yeah, I'd been *victimized*, but I sure as heck didn't like to think of myself as a victim. Finally, I tried on his words again. "What," I asked myself, "part did I play in being abducted?" I did not like what I saw. Even though I'd never admitted it to myself before, I did play a part in that *Defining Incident*; I played *the critical part* in that *Defining Incident*. The lie that was at the heart of all of the suffering around my *Defining Incident* was that someone else did this to me. Sure, those men did what they did, but before any of that happened, I knew I shouldn't have gone with them. There was no gray area there; in black-and-white terms, I knew I shouldn't have gone, period.

So, back to this tenet: you are responsible for everything that happens in your life. Everything. Getting this tenet down to your bones will set you free. Despite how you may feel about it, if you are willing to own this tenet, your life will never be the same. It may seem like a classic case of adding insult to injury to not only have something bad happen but to then be asked to claim responsibility for that bad thing happening. The one thing I've found, however, without exception, is that to the degree you're willing to claim responsibility for what happened, you will be free. And isn't it high time for that already?

Our human logic reasons that if we can duck responsibility for what happened; if we can place the blame squarely on someone or something else, anyone or anything else, really, then we'll be okay. Somehow the very action of naming someone or something else as the accountable party, we reason, will undo the bad that was done. Problem is, that's fundamentally flawed logic; what's done is done, and nothing or no one is going to reverse that and bring things back to the way they were before. Traditionally we don't want to see that, however, so we weave our tale of woe, complete with victims and aggressors, and "shoulda/woulda/coulda" scenarios, and we tell that tale to anyone who will listen. On the flip side, there are those people who don't breathe a word of their tale of woe to another soul; they suffer in silence. The end result is the same, though: the very act of bucking responsibility ensures that the experience of the bad, unfair things that happened in the past keep happening again and again, day after day, forever.

To free yourself, it's going to take making a leap in your interpretation of yourself and the circumstances which occurred; you will need to go from: there is a victim and an aggressor (and any hint of a "shoulda/woulda/coulda" scenario,) to instead that you and you alone are responsible for things happening in the way they happened.

It's worth noting that when I say, "take responsibility" I am not saying, "take the blame for," or, "are the guilty party," or any kind of disempowering interpretation of that nature including that you are bad, or that you should have known better. On the contrary, the act of "taking responsibility for" as I'm distinguishing it here is an entirely different notion; consider that it is the fundamental step in the process of alchemy; it is the key ingredient that will transmute you and your life from "lead" to "gold."

I know this tenet can be difficult to contend with and to confront; on more than one occasion, I've had sessions where clients ended their session prematurely during the discussion of this tenet rather than considering the possibility that they could have had any hand in what happened to them. If you are finding this a difficult proposition to stomach, console yourself with the fact that you are not alone. Taking on this tenet is contrary and opposite to the way human beings are wired. For what it's worth, this tenet is traditionally the most challenging tenet by far for people to implement, so if you're confronted, take to heart that you're in good company.

As counter-intuitive as it may sound, if you can *declare* responsibility; if you can *wrest* responsibility, if you can *seize* responsibility for all that happened, you'll be in the driver's seat of your life once again.

If you're unwilling to be responsible for the bad that happened in your life, you can't be responsible for the good or anything in-between that happens. You are then, by default, declaring that you are a victim of circumstance; you play the role of the victim in your own life; you are a pawn; you are like flotsam on the water, bandied about by fate; you are powerless. You may as well lie down and die now. Your only access to a life worth living is to be at cause rather than at effect of your existence; that step begins by owning the bad you've designed as well as the good and the in-between.

Take the case that at the heart of every "bad experience" or *Defining Incident* in life there is a lie; there is a truth not being told. A good "way in" in terms of starting the process of taking responsibility for everything in your life is to look for the lie, or to look for the truth that isn't being told.

In my case, the moment I looked for the lie, it was immediately visible; sure, I initially wanted to look away and not own it; owning the lie would mean I was responsible for being abducted. But hadn't I gone through the hell long enough of pretending I was a victim in the matter? Where had that outlook gotten me? Sure, I could have joined victim's support groups, and survivor's circles, but either of those "solutions" would have left me constantly tethered to being both a victim and a survivor; in other words, I'd forever be dragging around the abduction, the beating and the rape with me. And I'd had enough of doing that.

I looked for the lie, and here's what I saw: I knew I shouldn't have gone with the men in France. I knew I should have never gone to meet them at the restaurant. First of all, I'd made a solemn vow to my mother that I would not split up with my friend Lizzie. I had never in my life broken my word to my mother, and yet I did it then, anyway. That was lie number one. Lie number two was that Lizzie had insisted that I not go; she told me the guy was creepy, and she had a bad feeling about him, and she absolutely forbade me from going. I ignored her completely; I disregarded our friendship, and went anyway. Third and most importantly, I knew in my heart and soul that going was wrong. My intuition told me not to go, and even though I knew it was a bad idea, I went because I was so desperate to be a model.

I stared my lie straight in the face, and I just sat with it. I allowed myself to squirm and be uncomfortable, and my mind came up with all kinds of "Yeah, but…" conversations. I let those conversations come and go, then come and go again…repeatedly, until my mind finally stopped justifying. When it did, I found myself in the presence of a sense of calm and peacefulness that washed over me. The next thing I experienced was a sense of potency and power. I allowed all the feelings to well up and subside; I allowed it all. It all started, however, with the willingness to look for the lie in my *Defining Incident*.

The third tenet, if taken to heart, provides a contextual shift in the life of participant. Previous to incorporating *Tenet Number Three* into one's life, the locus of control exists externally, if a person is victimized in any way by their *Defining Incidents*. Because the control for that person's life is out of their hands, the possibility for their future remains bleak; they will likely remain exactly as they are: a victim. Once a person internalizes *Tenet Number Three* and volitionally shifts the locus of control for their life to being *internal*, suddenly that person has a say in how their life goes from that point forward.

To be clear, shifting the locus of control is an act of will; no one can force you to declare you are responsible for everything that happens in your life and no one can force another to make that choice. It is a choice of free will and can only occur voluntarily.

Once, however, a person authentically declares that they are responsible for everything that happened in their life and will ever happen in their life, that is the very moment they seize the reins and wrest control of their own life again. It is a remarkable and truly unique opportunity for being alive.

Have you ever heard the Pierre Teilhard de Chardin quote that states, "We are not human beings having a spiritual experience; we are spiritual beings having a human experience"?

That truly is a wonderful quote, one I believe is accurate. I think it's often taken too literally by people and used as a complete roadmap rather than as a light upon the path. Here's what I mean: I absolutely love the notion that at our core we are spiritual beings who are having a human incarnation, rather than being mere human beings who experience flickers of spiritual awakening. The problem often becomes that the story doesn't end there. This is particularly important for those people in the spiritual community or for those who are unwilling to do the work upon themselves.

Yes, it is an empowering context to declare for oneself that we are spiritual beings having a human experience, not the other way around, but even so, we are still human beings who must live and work and inhabit the physical realm. As such there are things for which we must be responsible. We have to handle our humanness before we can address our spirituality. Like it or not, our existence is limited to the physical realm; we can't escape it and check out; no matter how far "off the grid" you go, you're still confined by a body, a mind, and thoughts. No amount of meditation will handle your humanness; you'll still have that to deal with.

Have you ever had the experience of being sabotaged? Like as if no matter how much you want to change and how many great new plans you come up with and how excitedly you speak with others about those great new plans you end up right back where you were, or even worse, you're behind the point where you originally started? Can you relate? I say that's your humanness taking the reins. That's the point of this section: I assert that we must handle our humanness in order to live the lives to which we are committed.

The fact that we're "spiritual beings having a human experience," instead of it being the other way around, buys us nothing.

My mother is a yogi who has been traveling to India and teaching both the spiritual path and the physical path of yoga since 1969. As a result, I've grown up in what would be considered quite a spiritual environment. I've gone to spiritual workshops, retreats, and pilgrimages since I was a toddler; my brother, sister and I were trained to read auras before we could read the written word. I was reared reciting the ancient Sanskrit texts and chants; I know the Hindu deities as well as I know the Catholic saints. The teachings of Ernest Holmes were considered bedtime stories in our home. Suffice it to say, I'm familiar with spirituality. If that's taught me anything, it's that "being spiritual" buys me nothing; it doesn't handle my humanness in the least. I grapple with my humanness every day; I get derailed, disempowered and overtaken by the conversations in my head. The conversations in my head are something like Rose from the nursing home…on crack. I get inspired and lose that inspiration every day.

Being "spiritual" doesn't handle jack. On the contrary, some of the most so-called "spiritual" people I've ever met have a tenuous relationship to their humanness and therefore little relationship to reality as it truly exists. They'll argue with you, "That is not *my reality*," but Honey, I don't care *whose* reality it is; if the state of California says you have to obey x, y, or z law, and if you don't obey those laws they'll throw you in jail no matter if that's "your reality or not." If you don't pay your rent they will throw you out on the street no matter how many affirmations you say to the contrary.

My point: as beings who inhabit both the physical plane and human bodies, we have to handle our humanness. I'll presuppose you're addressing the basics of that already; you're handling your nutritional, health, and fitness needs, and you've got a roof over your head as well as whatever things you consider to be "basics" handled for yourself. In other words, in the teachings of Abraham Maslow and his "Hierarchy of Needs" model, I'll take it that you've already got your needs met in the areas of your biology, physiology, safety, etc. That being the case, we can move on to the so-called "higher" needs.

When I state that we need to handle our humanness, what I'm referring to is not those basic well-being needs I just mentioned; I'm referring to handling the mental and emotional aspects of our humanness.

In a moment I'll share with you a case study as an example of managing your humanness that I hope will provide you with some space to take this on like a game.

Chapter Twelve

Case Study Overview

From this point forward, I'm going to share with you several case studies from past and present clients and students. These case studies are intended to allow you to deepen your understanding about and application of the tenets at work.

There will be case studies of those who applied the work and succeeded; there will be stories of those who refused to apply the work, or do any kind of work on themselves at all, and the consequences of those choices. I think that following in the path of these clients and students—or not following their actions, as the case may be—will prove to be immensely valuable.

Reading the case studies where a person has completed the *Life Alchemy* journey will allow you to distinguish what a complete transmutation looks like: moving from a life given by a *Defining Incident* upward to zero, and then upward again in a second move to a life worth living.

Each of the clients featured has given me permission to use their story. Their names and identifying information have been changed.

Chapter Thirteen

Case Study: Barry

For nearly a year, I've been working with a client named Barry on running his business more efficiently and on creating and fulfilling goals for the company. Before long we started to work together on doing the same in Barry's personal life as well. Over the course of the past eleven months, we've systematically taken on the areas of life that are important to Barry, his family and his business. Recently Barry decided he wanted to tackle his nutrition and eating habits. While he's an athlete who runs marathons, he recently decided that his Cheetos, Peanut M & M's and Mountain Dew habit had to go. No one would know that Barry had a junk food habit; he is in such good shape that he burns off the calories in no time. That wasn't the problem for Barry, though; as we brought integrity to all of the other areas of his life, the junk food began to stand out for him as an area that he needed to eliminate. That was his idea, not mine; as I said, I'd never have even known about it had he not confessed it. The first two days went well; Barry established a diet and didn't cheat on it. He told his fiancée that he was cutting out all junk food, so she'd support him as well. Things seemed to be on track. That's when I got the call from Barry; it was before 8:00 a.m., and he was on his way to work.

"I stopped at a convenience store not once but twice yesterday. The first time was on the way back to the office before meeting with an unhappy client. He was stressed; I got stressed, and it was as if my car drove itself into the first 7-11 I saw. I ate one bag of Cheetos before I got to the cash register, turned around and grabbed another two and a Big Gulp. I inhaled all of it in the car before I even left the lot."

I listened as Barry went on.

"Last night," he started, "I took several clients out to the game. We had a couple of beers while we were there. I was sober by the time I drove home, but I was just more chilled out about things. I told myself that since I'd already broken my promise for the day, it didn't matter what I did now...again it was like my car pulled into the nearest convenience mart on its own. I got so much junk food that they gave me a shopping bag to hold it in. Do you know what a feat that is at a Chevron? I gorged myself on it within just a few miles. Then I felt so guilty and worried that Carolyn would see it in my car and find out, that I got up early enough this morning to go vacuum out my car before I pick her up tonight and take her to dinner, so she won't find out."

I let Barry know that I heard what he said; then he shouted out, "I feel like I'm trying to manage a five-year old!"

I told him that's because he is! That's very much what it's like to handle your humanness; it is like you're dealing with a five-year-old child! Can you relate? Have you ever taken action that is completely counter to what you say you're committed to? At the same time, have you found yourself immensely frustrated with yourself while you're in the very act of doing those things and yet felt powerless to do anything different? That's what I mean when I talk about dealing with your humanness. The exercises, processes and ideas that follow are designed to have you move from fighting your humanness to working along with it and engaging it to work with you to fulfill what you're up to, instead of having it working against you.

Barry and I had the following conversation, which I'd like you to try on for size.

I asked Barry to take the case that he was, in fact, managing a five-year-old. I asked him to imagine the scenario that he was the manager of a movie star, and that movie star happened to be five years old. If, I said, you were in fact managing a five-year-old and your livelihood relied upon that, you would allow for and make concessions for certain things. You'd put certain structures in place. For example, you'd ensure the child had a strict bedtime, and you'd make sure that he wasn't allowed to hang out at the snack table and eat as much sugar as he liked. You'd make sure that there would be someone on location to educate the child during the waiting times, so that he could keep up with whatever learning he'd need and not simply play video games or watch TV all day.

"Yeah. I'd make sure he had nap time, too," Barry added, jumping into imagining the scenario for himself.

I wasn't so much interested in *what* Barry would create, but that he got the concept that if he were truly "managing a five-year-old", he'd make certain concessions with and for that five-year-old child.

"But you didn't do that for yourself regarding your diet, did you?" I asked.

Barry said that he did not.

Mind you, this is a disciplined guy, for Pete's sake. He owns a successful sales company; he runs marathons; he honors his word. Tackling an area of life where he'd always done whatever he wanted was not easy for him, however. So I asked him to speculate on what kind of structures he'd create to have him fulfill this goal of cutting out all junk food if he looked at himself from the perspective of "managing a five-year-old."

Barry and I brainstormed for a few minutes and came up with several possibilities:

- He'd ensure he ate good food regularly, and that he had healthy snacks in his car.

- He'd pick up the phone and call someone if he was thinking about going on a junk food binge. First, however, he'd create a solid group of people on whom he could count to hold him accountable if he should ever call them in a moment of need.

- If he ever broke down again, he'd tell the truth about it, rather than trying to hide it and cover it up.

- He'd create a consequence and reward system to keep himself on track. For every day that Barry went without junk food he got to apply $100 toward the purchase of a new "toy." He had his eye on a new sports car, but couldn't seem to rationalize the purchase of it until he concocted this plan. For every day that Barry broke down and ate junk food, he had to take $500 out of his sports car fund.

As you continue your exploration into and work with the third tenet, "You Are Responsible For Everything That Happens In Your Life. Everything," play around with the concept of "managing a five-year-old" for yourself, and see if you can't use it to create a partnership with your "five-year-old" that's running the show.

Chapter Fourteen

Case Study: Peter

I worked with Peter in a professional capacity; I'd been brought in to work with him after a less-than-favorable performance review he'd been given by his higher-ups at work. Already a low-level executive in his company, Peter had a great potential to rise up the ranks. Peter had a great education; he was a natural problem solver; he was competent, and he was motivated. Peter's company saw his potential, which is why they invested the time and money in having me come in to work with him. The problem was, his review stated, Peter wasn't fulfilling his potential; he was not even coming close to doing so.

My intention was to remove whatever obstructions were impeding Peter from being the asset to his company and the man he was capable of being. When I started working with Peter, I asked him for permission to discuss his personal life; he said that was fine. I knew that addressing what was going on in his personal life was going to help me access whatever it was that needed to change in his business life.

Let's face it: as much as we might try to compartmentalize our lives, we are one being, with one life. There's no getting around it. If something isn't working in one "compartment" of our lives, it affects all the other "compartments." At one time or another, I'm sure we'd all prefer to be able to be submarine-like and have the ability to truly seal off one compartment from the others, but that's just not the way human beings are built.

In the first session with Peter, something fundamental arose in conversation immediately. Within the first few minutes, Peter brought up the fact that as a child he had been sexually abused by his priest.

I began to "connect the dots" immediately. The issue I'd been hired to solve first was the difficulty Peter was having with his higher-ups; reportedly Peter verged on being downright indignant with anyone who had to manage him; he was distrusting and disdainful about anyone in power.

It's not hard to imagine how Peter ended up that way; after all, in some context, his priest was the higher-up of the church who used to "manage" Peter back when he was an altar boy.

The problem was those events with Peter's priest occurred decades ago; they weren't happening now. Today there were just higher-ups trying to accomplish their jobs, and Peter was standing in their way. Peter was "virtually unmanageable" in the words of one report. He only held the job because of his potential and because of the difficulty the company saw in replacing him.

Peter belonged to a lot of support groups, and in fact he ran a lot of support groups. He frequently organized Meet-Up groups for other survivors of sexual abuse. Peter regularly spoke at meetings for Adult Survivors of Child Abuse, Al-Anon, and various advocacy groups whose mission was to prosecute and remove from the ministry current and past priests who were known or suspected sexual predators.

Peter's reading material consisted solely of books, articles or publications that dealt with the subject of sexual abuse, recovery from sexual abuse, or putting an end to sexual abuse and sexual abusers.

In our first session, Peter admitted to having sought therapy after the sexual abuse; he'd worked regularly with a therapist for eleven years.

"What I accomplished in therapy," Peter said, puffing out his chest, "is that I am no longer a victim. I can proudly say now that I am a survivor."

That was clear; Peter kept a solitary personal item in his office: it was a large framed parchment paper with the hand-written word, "SURVIVOR" written on it. The large frame hung prominently behind Peter's desk so that anyone who entered Peter's office could see it. As a matter of fact it was—quite intentionally—the only thing that visitors to Peter's office could see.

What wasn't clear, to Peter, at least, is that being a victim and being a survivor are essentially the same thing. Being both a victim and a survivor are predicated upon being firmly tethered to the past by a traumatizing event, and being personally identified with the event itself. Victim and survivor are simply different sides of the same coin.

There is a lot of importance in our culture placed upon survivor status; there are T-shirts, necklaces, bumper stickers, wall-hangings and more that advertise to the world that you survived cancer, incest, drug abuse, rape, or a suicide attempt. In this day and age, the world will laud you with support, smiles, accolades, and sympathy for proclaiming your survivor status. The predicament that survivor status presents is that when one personally identifies oneself with the event, circumstance or disease that one has survived, one is forever bound to that event, circumstance or disease. The traumatic event never goes away for the survivor; the traumatic event, out of necessity, must forever remain in the present moment. If the event slipped into the past where it belonged, there'd be no claiming survivorship possible. The ultimate irony of being a survivor is that one must continue surviving the traumatic incident, day after day, year after year, forever more.

I personally had no interest in being a survivor of abduction, physical abuse and rape; the event itself was horrific enough the first time; the last thing I want to do is identify myself with it by dragging it around with me in the present moment. The only time I ever mention it to another person is when I'm intentionally "giving it away" by speaking about what happened for the specific purpose of providing for another, the lesson for which it allowed.

As always, when I started working with Peter, I suggested that he start by declaring himself responsible for his life. He was furious about the prospect, despite how thoroughly I distinguished the difference between him taking responsibility and the *Defining Incident* being his fault. I suggested to Peter that while he was getting an immense amount of good will and sympathy from people—in addition to the acclaim he got from speaking at his various support groups—he was still stuck in the past. I asserted to Peter that developmentally we get stuck at the age that we were during our *Defining Incidents,* and that this left Peter with the problem of having limited competencies and abilities in that area while attempting to live his life as an adult everywhere else.

Peter was unwilling to consider any of this. He was unwilling to take responsibility for any aspect of his life. He kept coming back to the same thing, which, in one session he shouted aloud, "What Father John did to me was wrong, do you hear me? That was wrong! That should never have happened! No child should be subjected to that!"

While Peter is correct about that—absolutely no one in their right mind would argue that point—the fact that Peter is unwilling to let it go doesn't hurt Father John or any of the other sexual predators; it only hurts Peter. Peter is continuing to be abused; only now the abuse is being perpetrated by Peter himself.

Before long, Peter was being the same way with me as he was being with his supervisors: he was indignant, distrustful and disdainful. He outright refused to do the assignments I gave him or to work with me in the way my educational model is designed.

In a way, I can see why Peter chose to remain the way he was; he had concocted this perfect little reality where nobody would engage with him; nobody would dare "go there" with him; nobody would hold him to account for anything. His superiors came in his office to request something or give him constructive criticism; Peter would pull his, "How dare you ask me to do that? Don't you think I've suffered enough?!" routine on them, and they'd back down, one by one.

By the time I was called in, no one wanted to deal with him; that's why he was termed "virtually unmanageable." I truly believe I was the only person who ever went toe-to-toe with Peter. On the two occasions I told him I refused to be bought off with his "survivor" act he stormed out of his office and physically left our session. The second time he did so was his last; I removed myself from being his coach.

In one sense I can say, "I wonder what ever happened to Peter?" But what's unfortunate is I do know. In a literal sense, I know he no longer works for that company, but in a practical sense I know what happened to him on more than a work level. You, as the reader "know" as well…you can't help but know. Human beings are predictable; if you want to know who we're going to be in the future look at how we're being now. It's a no-brainer. Until Peter is willing to give up the "trophy" of being a survivor, he'll never have the real prize of having a life he loves.

Chapter Fifteen

Case Study: Thomas

Thomas came to me because he was undergoing a career transition. For years Thomas had been a firefighter in New York City, in fact he was a 9-11 First Responder. Since then he'd moved to California and had gone into the business of providing personal security. When he came to me, Thomas was in the process of hiring other people to handle the day-to-day security staffing, and setting himself up to run the operations of the business while maintaining a small group of select clients for himself.

Although Thomas had a solid vision for himself and his company, he was having difficulty implementing that plan. At our first session, Thomas admitted that he was contemplating just scrapping the entire plan and moving back to New York again. He was burned out and was having some health problems that he'd incurred during the actual 9-11 event. He also confided that his relationships with women were so bad he limited himself to anonymous sex and prostitutes in order to avoid emotional connection of any kind with women.

As with every client, I quickly got into the business of requesting that Thomas take responsibility for everything that was in his life—including 9-11 itself. That is a radical concept; I know; how on earth could anyone possibly take responsibility for a massive, globally impacting, act of terrorism like that? There are unquestionably those people who would insist that I'm insensitive at best and out of my mind at worst. Insensitive and out of my mind or not, there's one thing of which I'm certain: the act of declaring oneself responsible in the matter leaves one firmly seated at the controls of one's own life in the way nothing else can.

Thomas was unwilling to consider that proposition.

He'd hired me for a reason, though, so I stepped up and challenged him to participate with me in order to cause the result he'd come to me to produce. I suggested that he consider that he wore being a 9-11 first responder like a badge.

He spoke up immediately saying, "You're damn right; I do!"

I explained to him that wasn't a good thing. Don't get me wrong; being a 9-11 First Responder was a brave, noble, courageous thing to do. We Americans owe Thomas and everyone else who performed that work a debt of gratitude. That's not my point. My point is this: Thomas defines himself as a 9-11 First Responder and as a 9-11 First Responder alone. It's no wonder he's having difficulty creating anything new in his life.

The fact that he is a 9-11 First Responder is something Thomas says to people immediately upon meeting them. He intentionally works that fact into each and every conversation, and that fact has people relating to Thomas as a hero. That's pretty heady stuff, you have to admit; just imagine if everywhere you went people related to you as a hero, thanked you, took your photo, listened raptly when you spoke and wept at your tales. There truly is no wonder that Thomas was unwilling to give up that payoff.

When I suggested to Thomas that his need to be perceived, in every moment, as a hero was keeping him from living the life he truly wanted, he shook his head and refused to look me in the eye. We sat in silence until he finally suggested we end our session.

I have the utmost compassion for Thomas; the very reason why most of us create and attempt to fulfill goals and dreams in the first place is so that eventually people will relate to us in the exact way that they relate to Thomas right now. The problem is that his need to be related to as a hero has Thomas needing to drag around with him the experience of 9-11. He experiences the horror of that day every day. I know that because he told me so; he said 9-11 never leaves him. Many of Thomas' health problems are a direct result of the fact that he cannot sleep. He is plagued by the images and visions of that day from hell; those images and visions haunt him day and night. The design flaw to his "perfect plan" of being a hero in everyone's eyes is that he has to re-live 9-11 every day, day after day, without end.

On the most basic and pragmatic of levels, one way Thomas re-lives the event every day is that he engages with people daily who ask him to explain what the event was like. It is as if Thomas wears a sign around his neck reading, "Ask me everything you've always wanted to know about 9-11!" As Thomas recounts the event, he divulges every gory and gruesome detail with gusto; his audience is always the same: wide-eyed, horrified, and yet oddly enraptured. They cry along with him; they thank him; they are in awe of him. One constant each time Thomas recounts the 9-11 tale is that he tells the listeners how bad his health is as a result. From persistent lung problems, to ruptured disks, to a complete inability to sleep without powerful prescription medicine (and the ensuing fallout from that) Thomas always brings up his poor health. Each time the listeners express their sympathy, gratitude, and care.

I've heard the entire 9-11 story from Thomas on three separate occasions when we have been out in public together; each event was with strangers. It was emotionally draining and exhausting for me just to listen to; I can't imagine how emotionally draining and exhausting it is for Thomas to recount.

Once again, I pressed in with Thomas to take responsibility for the event and for his life. I asked him to start with taking responsibility for just one tiny part of it. I let him know he didn't need to start with taking responsibility for the whole enchilada; any small piece of responsibility that he was willing to claim would provide freedom and open up the space for him to move forward. I assured him that if he did even that and took responsibility for a small part of what happened, eventually it would allow him to fulfill what he came to me to fulfill.

Thomas was unwilling to do so. At first he pretended he was willing to do so but in the end he was not. At the end of each session, I'd give him an assignment; each week he'd return to his following session not having completed any of the assignments. Ultimately I had to stop working with him.

What's illustrated so well in the example of Thomas is how we human beings so often say we want something different than we have in our life, and we complain about the circumstances we have in our lives right now. Thomas complained vociferously about the fact that he couldn't seem to get his career working, that he couldn't find reliable staff, that he hated L.A., that his relationships with women were horrible, and that his health was suffering,

Thomas claimed that he wanted a new, fresh life with a flourishing business, great health and a fulfilling relationship and marriage, but he was unwilling to even consider that it was his attachment to living in the past that was keeping him from having the life he wanted in the present.

For Thomas, being regarded as a hero was a massive win; he was unwilling to let go of that recognition and appreciation and worship from others. I asserted to him that he could be recognized, appreciated and loved for who he is, not what he's done, but he was afraid to let go of the shore for fear he'd never reach the other side. It's funny; Thomas is the last person you'd ever think of as a fearful person; I mean, this is a man who performed acts of courage and bravery that most people could never fathom performing, and yet, ultimately, it was his fear that trapped him.

Another problem that Thomas didn't foresee is that there will be diminishing returns for him in being recognized as a hero as 9-11 fades in people's memory. Over time Thomas will get less and less from telling that story; there will be fewer accolades, sparser acclaim, and less hero worship. Thomas will have to work harder and harder to have people feel sympathy for him, or admire him, or think him heroic. By design, Thomas will have to, over time, become more and more of a victim to get the same result. He has effectively created his own prison.

Thomas truly could have created being regarded as a hero anywhere he went if he simply put his mind to it. The design flaw with the world that he concocted is he has to be a victim, and he has to be hurting and injured to be regarded as a hero. He has to lose in order to win in this game.

The tragedy for me about Thomas is that he is a vibrant, vivacious, charismatic, handsome, intelligent man that could have people eating out of his hand to listen to any story he chose to tell. I am just sorry that the story he does choose to tell will never provide that for which he most deeply longs in life.

TENET NUMBER FOUR:

You Will Never Be Happy or Fulfilled

Until You Are The Architect of Your Life. ™

Chapter Sixteen

Tenet Number Four:

You Will Never Be Happy or Fulfilled Until You Are The Architect of Your Life.

"There are some people who live in a dream world, and there are some who face reality; and then there are those who turn one into the other."
-Douglas H. Everett

This tenet requires a leap. So in order to bring you into the process with some ease and grace I want to start this chapter with a parable.

Have you ever heard the story about God wanting to experience Himself? There are several different variations of this parable that I've heard told over the years; here is my own. I call it *The Story of Everything*. It is designed to give you a different point-of-view on your human existence.

There's a parable that says that in the beginning there was nothing but God, which is to say that all that existed was Every-thing and No-

thing. Everything was at peace there, surrounded by nothing, but after a few million years, the parable goes on to say, that since there was nothing for Everything to do and nothing to interact with, Everything got lonely and bored. So Everything created the heavens and the Earth and all the planets and the galaxy. A few million years later, Everything was back in that same space of being lonely and bored again, so Everything decided to play a game. Everything wanted to experience life outside of Him/Herself; the only way Everything could see to do that was to splinter off into billions of little pieces. Then, Everything surmised, He/She could experience "another." The catch was, Everything realized, that Everything was going to have to hide from the pieces that they were all "Everything" at their core; after all, how much fun is it to interact with only oneself forever? Everything already knew the answer from only having Him/Herself to interact with for millions upon millions of years: it was not much fun at all.

So the game was that Everything would splinter off into billions of little pieces and hide from each piece that they were all the same, and they were part of the whole. Then, in order to make the game even more interesting— and you have to remember how much Everything was just longing for interesting at this point—the game would go on for as long as it took for every single solitary one of the billions of little pieces to remember who they were and to return home to the whole.

"It may take lifetime, upon lifetime, upon lifetime, for those billions of little pieces of me to remember who they are and return home," Everything thought, "but that's what'll make this an engaging, exciting game! What good is a game if everyone figures it out early because it's easy? I need a game," Everything thought, "that can be played for eons."

So Everything created the Big Bang and split into billions of little pieces, each one of them containing the perfect hologram of the whole, and each one being formed from the substance of Everything as the core of their being— although, again, the game was that each piece had to remain unaware of that fact. Before they descended upon the Earth, the billions of little pieces gathered together with Everything and they spoke about the game with such enthusiasm

122

and excitement they could barely contain themselves. They finalized the rules of the game and defined the ways that they could win and return home. The billions of little pieces wanted to make sure they had a game worth playing as well, so they decided to make it really interesting and compelling for themselves.

"We'll pretend to be different," one of them suggested as several of them burst into laughter.

"However will we do that?" Another one asked, adding, "We're all the same. We come from the same source; we're made up of the same source; I am you as you are me."

"We'll make our outsides different," someone suggested, "As well as our beliefs and our habits and our cultures!"

Several cheers were let out by the crowd.

"But best of all," Everything reminded, "You'll have no memory of us having this meeting; you'll forget completely who you are!"

They all burst into wild applause at that one. Little pieces banded together with other pieces and agreed to be families and countries and races. Excited, happy conversations broke out amongst all of the billions of little pieces.

"I'll pretend to be your enemy, and I'll kill you and your whole family," one little piece said to another.

"Why would you do that?" A third little piece asked.

The first little piece smiled and said, "Because I love him, of course, and I want to give him the best game possible!"

They all laughed, hugged, and understood.

"It'll be my turn to play the bad guy the next go-around!" Another one of them said, and the others agreed.

Everything interrupted all of their planning and spoke. "How you'll win the game is to remember who you are when you are on Earth. The veils of illusion on your new planet will be very strong; while you are on Earth you will be tempted to think that what you perceive with your senses is real; it will not be. Only what you sense deep in your heart will be real. If you are able to pierce the veils of illusion and see perfection in the middle of your incarnation on Earth, you will win, and you can return home to the whole. Once each and every one of you has remembered who you are and can see the perfection even while in human form on Earth, the game will be over, and we can choose a new game to play."

"But Father," one of the pieces asked, "Can we choose to stay on Earth once we are awakened?"

Everything smiled. "That would certainly add a new level of play to the game, now, wouldn't it, My Child."

"Yes, it would." The little piece responded. "I could help awaken my brothers and sisters and assist them in returning home."

"There are billions of you," Everything said, "so I can imagine the only way this game would ever end is if each one of you helped awaken each other in some fashion."

They all sat in silence, anticipating the beginning of the game.

"So that is my charge to you, My Beloveds. Go to Earth; forget who you are, and help awaken each other when you get there."

"But Father," another one interrupted, "how will we be able to awaken each other if the veils of illusion are as strong on Earth as you've said they are?"

Everything beamed. "Good question, My Child. Each of you will be given gifts that are uniquely yours. It will be your job to locate those gifts— they may not come packaged as gifts at all, which is just part of the game—and give those gifts away to others. Using and giving your gifts fully is what will awaken you and what will help to awaken all.

"Go forth, My Children," Everything said, "and remember: it's only a game."

Again, *Tenet Number Four* is "You Will Never Be Happy or Fulfilled Until You Are The Architect of Your Life." Your key to having whatever you consider to be a life worth living is to be the architect of your existence. That begins by first taking responsibility for the life of which you've already been the architect, even if you previously designed your life unconsciously. Your next step in becoming the architect of your life is to declare for yourself that the life you have had up until this point has been perfect. Until you can authentically create that what you've had to deal with is a blessing, you will never be able to be a *Life Architect*. This especially applies to the most challenging, difficult, or traumatic events you've faced.

There are two parts to this tenet:

1. Realizing that you already *have* been the architect of your life, you've just been doing so unconsciously.

2. Consciously set about being the architect of your life and designing an existence about which you are thrilled.

Essentially becoming the architect of your life requires another level in taking responsibility for your life; this next level takes a leap in thinking, however. There's a principle in metaphysics that states that a person is a co-creator, along with The Universe/God, of their life. If that's true, then each person is responsible on a macro level for absolutely everything that occurs in their incarnation, including their parents, their race, place of birth, every situation that has ever happened to them, their financial success or poverty, their handicaps, abilities, and disabilities...all of it.

When we can authentically make that declaration for ourselves and truly name every circumstance and event as a blessing, then we will truly be life alchemists and transform all of the "lead" in our lives into "gold." In that moment, we come into the presence of the profound privilege of being alive.

It is a massive step for a person to move from being traumatized and negatively impacted by a *Defining Incident* to get back to "zero." In no way do I mean to diminish the enormity of that act. To move from "wounded" to "okay" and not stop at "survivor" is more than most people achieve in a lifetime.

Initially, in my own journey, I thought the point was simply that one step: moving from "wounded" to "okay." But something was missing. No one dreams of living a life of "okay." "Okay" is mediocre and uninspiring. Sure, It's a step up from "wounded" or "victimized" or being at the effect of life, but it's ordinary and pedestrian. I realized that my own journey and struggle to become "okay" with the abduction would be pretty hollow if I stopped at "okay."

It was by accident that I realized there were two parts to *Life Alchemy*. As I mentioned, at first I thought there was just the first step of returning to "zero" or "okay." Because it seemed for me that something was still missing; the process was still incomplete. I grappled with that for a while. As I began to ponder the nature of alchemy, it hit me that there were two moves that comprised the *Life Alchemy Method,* and the second upward move is as essential as the first. The second upward move is also equivalent in distance as the first upward move.

It was when working with a client named Vincent that I formally distinguished the two steps that comprise *The Life Alchemy Method.* I'd been employing both steps in my life for some time; I simply hadn't distinguished the two upward steps as "the two upward steps" yet. In a moment, I'll share Vincent's story with you.

In my own example, the first step was that I took responsibility for and resolved the issue of the abduction. I recognized how I'd been hauling that issue around with me everywhere in order to survive, and I was able to completely let it go. That brought me to "okay." Some part of the puzzle was still incomplete and unresolved, however; there was still further upward to travel.

When I was working with my client Vincent on the process of having him take responsibility for and be resolved about having been in a life-threatening car accident, something started to open up. Something started to emerge that tied the final step of the method to naming the occurrence a blessing, and therefore to transmute the entire *Defining Incident* into a blessing. That's what I'd been doing when I decided to give my story away; watching Vincent go through the same process had me distinguish the process that was happening.

As I mentioned, I'll share about Vincent's alchemical journey later; for now I'll distinguish more of the alchemical process using my own example. In the *Life Alchemy Method* there is an equally gigantic leap from being victimized by a *Defining Incident* to taking responsibility for it, as there is from having taken responsibility for it, to naming that *Defining Incident* a blessing.

I went from first being destroyed by the fact that I had been abducted, beaten, and raped, to "being okay" with it, then finally on to embracing it and authentically saying, "This is the best thing that ever happened in my life. This *Defining Incident* is the very thing that allowed me to lead seminars, become a coach and connect with people I wouldn't have otherwise met. It's allowed me to become an author and be able to have my life make a difference."

Taking this action truly allowed me to transmute the remaining "lead" in my life into "gold." There's a difference between not being upset about the hand you were dealt in life and having that very hand you were dealt be the factor that gives the most extraordinary life that you could ever have fathomed. This tenet is your access to living that life.

If you'll recall from earlier, I mentioned that we need to first handle our humanness before we can address our spirituality. That is another way that one could explain "the two steps":

- Step One: handle your humanness.
- Step Two: address (unleash or create) your spirituality.

By the way, when I use the term "spirituality", I'm not talking about some chanting baloney, or some lofty concepts, or living in a cave, or getting a guru, or changing your name to Sanskrit, or becoming a vegetarian. I'm talking about the deep, primal longing that each of us has to matter, to impact other people, to embody and live our highest vision for our own lives and to have our being here make some lasting difference.

I do not believe that to be a spiritual person you can't drink, fight, raise your voice, swear, have sex, etc. My point is that you integrate that which is timeless and eternal into this moment, and you live the dichotomy between being human while simultaneously being an embodiment of The Divine.

Once I witnessed Vincent naming his near-death accident the best thing that ever happened to him, and seeing that doing so made all of the difference in his life. I identified what I'd been doing all along. Until that moment, I didn't previously realize that our *Defining Incidents* themselves were the ticket to everything we'd ever wanted.

Chapter Seventeen

Case Study: Vincent

Vincent was a successful attorney; he was a partner at one of the large Los Angeles law firms. His father was an attorney; his grandfather was an attorney; that was simply what there was for Vincent to do; he had to be an attorney. Or so he thought.

Vincent came to me through a referral. Despite the fact that he was immensely successful on the surface, he hated his work, and he hated his life.

We had a couple of rushed sessions. There were always "fires" for Vincent to put out at work; he'd made himself indispensable. We had another two sessions scheduled, but Vincent had to cancel both of them because—you guessed it—something came up at work. He paid for the sessions he canceled but I was frustrated because I knew I could make a difference for Vincent and the quality of his life.

Vincent promised me we'd get back to working together soon, but "soon" just kept getting pushed further and further away.

One night on the way home from an exceptionally late night at work, a drunk driver hit Vincent head on. Vincent was taken by ambulance to the ER; once there he was rushed into urgent brain surgery where he remained for close to seven hours. Rather than emerging from brain surgery healed, Vincent slipped into a coma where he remained for nearly a week.

When Vincent finally regained consciousness, his physicians gave him a pessimistic prognosis. They didn't expect him to ever walk again; they said he'd have permanent problems of an unknown nature due to the severity of his brain injury; Vincent also suffered hearing loss, memory loss and a complete loss of his senses of smell and taste.

Vincent slipped in and out of consciousness for days. The last interaction Vincent remembered was the meeting with his doctors, and their words stayed on his mind. Before he slipped away, Vincent vowed to himself that if he made it through this incident, he'd quit being an attorney and move to Maui to become an artist as he'd always wanted to do.

When he finally returned to being permanently conscious, Vincent made good on the promise he made to himself. He informed the other partners at the firm that he was hanging up his hat and giving up law for good.

"I knew I could always return to law someday if I really needed to, but I was resolved to never need to," Vincent later said.

There were those colleagues, friends, and family members of Vincent who were sure that he'd lost his mind in the accident. "What they didn't realize," he said, "is that for the first time I could recall, I'd actually found my mind!"

Vincent sold his house in Los Angeles and moved to Maui. Once there, Vincent got about the business of physical therapy; he worked for months to be able to walk again, and he succeeded.

Throughout this period, Vincent and I had several coaching sessions via phone; he never missed a one. It was profoundly fulfilling to be with this man during the process of him becoming the architect of his life.

Toward the end of his intensive physical therapy, Vincent started painting again.

"Do you know I haven't held a brush in my hands for over two decades?" he said, filled with a sense of pride. "Thank God that person ran into me that night," he said, recalling his accident. "If I'd been listening to myself more closely, perhaps he wouldn't have had to have injured me quite so badly to get my attention," he joked. "But who am I to complain? That accident was the best thing that ever happened to me."

He took over one of the guest bedrooms as a studio, then before long had workers come to his home to tear down the wall between the two guest bedrooms and make the space into one huge studio. At the moment, he's considering finding a larger house with a larger space to paint. There's also a special woman in his life now, and he wants to ensure that she'll have space of her own in the house.

Every single time Vincent and I speak he says the same thing when asked the question, "How are you?" His response is always identical:

"Better than oughtta be legal!"

Vincent is well on the way to a complete transmutation in terms of the process of *Life Alchemy*; after his *Defining Incident* he moved up not only to "okay," but upward still to becoming the architect of his life and designing an existence that he loves. In *Tenet Number Five*, you'll learn the final step in the *Life Alchemy Method*; the one that has a person accomplish a complete transmutation of their life.

Chapter Eighteen

Case Study: Maddy

When Maddy came to me she was a woman who was emotionally scarred from having been through a very difficult divorce from Ron, who had been her high school sweetheart once upon a time. The couple had married right after graduation; they'd been together the greater part of their lives. Maddy and Ron had two children and fought an angry, bitter custody battle over them. Maddy considered that battle to be the final straw.

"I just didn't know how I'd ever move on," Maddy said during our first session with her eyes welling up with tears.

Unfortunately, Maddy didn't have much time to ponder the question of how she'd move on; she was forced into action when she quickly learned that the spousal support and child support payments she was awarded were nowhere near enough to pay for what she and the kids needed.

After working a couple of soul-killing jobs for little to no pay, Maddy felt worse off than ever. That's when the idea came to her.

"I was in the kitchen baking a fresh berry pie for my best friend's birthday when a bolt hit me smack between the eyes: I may not have many skills, but I damn sure can bake!"

Maddy knew a couple of business investors through friends of friends. She called them and pitched the idea of opening her own bakery. They were not moved. She was desperate and not worried about how she'd come off, so Maddy baked up all of her favorites and marched them straight into the office of the investor pair. They couldn't believe how delectable Maddy's baked goods were—neither could their staff who kept running in for more—the investors agreed on the spot to contribute the start-up capital for Maddy to open a small bake shop.

"It wasn't the best area of town; I wasn't getting the best percentage of earnings, and there were no guarantees I'd even get one customer, but it was mine, and I was working for myself. That was a dream come true."

Maddy worked tirelessly for years to make the bakery flourish, which it did. She brought on staff and searched for ways to expand her customer base. Eventually Maddy returned to the method that originally had proven so successful; she baked up her goodies and personally marched them into various restaurants and coffee shops around town. Again, people could not believe how delicious her desserts were, and again, they became customers.

Maddy now has two stores in operation, and her business is booming.

When Maddy and I began working together, I was most interested in why her marriage and divorce from Ron still had so much sting to it. It had been so many years now since they'd divorced that Ron had re-married, and her kids were grown and out of the house. But the pain for Maddy was still there.

As usual, we started by having Maddy confront what she could take responsibility for in the divorce. I posed the question; then we sat silently for a minute, the two of us, in Maddy's kitchen. Then without a word, Maddy got up, went into to her refrigerator and cupboards and started whipping something up. A minute or so later, she looked up and looked me straight in the eye.

"I'm completely checked out, aren't I?" she said, smiling feebly.

I nodded understandingly to her with love and compassion filling my heart.

Maddy wiped her hands, put the perishables away and came and sat in front of me again.

"I stopped caring. That showed up in a lot of ways; I let the house go; I let the passion in my marriage go; I let myself go."

I listened intently as Maddy went on.

"Seriously, though. I know I've said that Ron is the world's biggest ass. It's true that he did things that only an ass would do, but he wasn't in this alone. He wasn't the only transgressor. I don't think I'd had sex with the man in over six months. Six months! Who can blame him for cheating? Don't get me wrong; I don't condone his behavior for a second, but he didn't operate in a vacuum."

She paused for a moment, but she seemed on the brink of saying more. She looked away for a moment, and then looked me squarely in the eye.

"I was a hundred pounds overweight. Closer to two hundred, if I tell the truth about it. And the worst part wasn't my weight; it was how righteous I was about it. It was as if I was daring him to leave me...as if I was making him prove that he loved me enough to stay."

Maddy took several deep breaths then finally spoke again. "I've always said that Ron is the biggest manipulator I know. That's not true; I've got that man beat by a mile in the manipulation game."

I was moved by Maddy's generosity; not everyone is willing to take responsibility for their part in the matter of the circumstances in their lives. To do so is truly an act of generosity and is the first essential step in the process of being a life alchemist.

Before long Maddy, Ron and Ron's wife Trish started gathering together at special occasions. Whether it was one of the kids' birthdays or a holiday, they all spent it together and did so without fighting. That was a huge improvement over the past. I knew there was another level possible for them, though.

I gave Maddy several exercises to do so she could finally and completely heal any remaining hurts from her relationship with Ron.

In our follow-up session, Maddy said she had done all of the exercises, and that they changed the way she related to Ron. Previously she'd related to him as her ex-husband and the person who fathered her children.

"I realized that interpretation itself is what has our relationship be stunted and never move beyond the cordial. From now on I'm going to relate to Ron as what he really is: my family. Same goes for Trish."

Maddy continued, "The moment I truly accepted the whole situation as a blessing, I immediately tapped into the love I had with Ron...it was the first time I'd felt love toward him in years. I realized I love this man with all my heart, but I also realized that loving him with all my heart does not mean I want to be his wife, or I want him to be my husband; it simply means I am no longer going to kill the love I have for him and replace it with hate to make it easier to deal with that I have love there that is...unused...so to speak."

A miraculous thing occurred for Maddy once she had completed a forgiveness process with the mental image of Ron; the real Ron called her the next day and wanted to meet. He suggested they go out for a drink; it was the first time the pair had gone out since being divorced. The drinks turned into dinner, which turned into the two of them closing the restaurant down. They recounted everything, re-lived a lot of moments, and forgave all.

When Maddy was free to experience and express that, Ron followed suit. They both realized they had an immense love for one another; that love had just changed forms. Now their love wasn't characterized by being married.

Another miraculous result happened for Maddy: she met a man and fell in love. She and James met at a coffee shop that sells her baked goods. She had literally just stopped in there one day while browsing on the street for antiques with a girlfriend, and met James while waiting for the restroom.

It's been over seven months for Maddy and James, and things are looking better than ever. Maddy and Ron's kids love James; James, Ron and Trish get along famously, and Maddy is still absolutely giddy whenever James does something sweet for her—which is daily.

Maddy says without hesitation that getting divorced from Ron was the best thing that ever happened to her. "If that didn't happen, I'd never have been pushed to discover myself...to create myself...to fulfill who I'd always wanted to be, but never believed I had it in me to be.

The divorce was the 'cosmic shove' that pushed me out of the nest, and it made me learn how to fly," she says.

TENET NUMBER FIVE:

You Only Get to Keep What You Give Away ™

Chapter Nineteen

Tenet Number Five:

You Only Get To Keep What You Give Away

"All of us are born for a reason, but all of us don't discover why. Success in life has nothing to do with what you gain in life or accomplish for yourself. It's what you do for others."

-Danny Thomas

Would you like to be in love? You know, that make-you-melt, curl your toes, get-you-outta-bed-in-the-morning kind of love? Better get used to it; that kind of love is never going to hunt you down and show up on your doorstep one morning. Love will never alight on you; love is something you have to first be open to, then generate, and then give away. It's like the beautiful quote from Elbert Hubbard that says, "Love grows by giving. The love we give away is the only love we keep. The only way to retain love is to give it away.

Want love? Give love. Want peace-of-mind? Provide peace-of-mind. Want riches? Bestow riches.

The fifth and final tenet in this series is based on the "Pay It Forward" theory; first promulgated by Benjamin Franklin in his letter to Benjamin Webb dated April 22, 1784. The letter was written by Franklin while in Passy, France, where he lived for nine years during the American Revolutionary War. While there in Passy—which years later would become a part of Paris—Franklin both worked on his scientific projects in a laboratory and established a small printing press. The particular letter in question was written because Franklin was lending Webb some money. The letter reads,

Dear Sir,

I received yours of the 15th Instant, and the Memorial it inclosed. The account they give of your situation grieves me. I send you herewith a Bill for Ten Louis d'ors. I do not pretend to give such a Sum; I only lend it to you.

When you shall return to your Country with a good Character, you cannot fail of getting into some Business, that will in time enable you to pay all your Debts. In that Case, when you meet with another honest Man in similar Distress, you must pay me by lending this Sum to him; enjoining him to discharge the Debt by a like Operation, when he shall be able, and shall meet with another opportunity.

I hope it may thus go thro' many hands, before it meets with a Knave that will stop its Progress. This is a trick of mine for doing a deal of good with a little money. I am not rich enough to afford much in good works, and so am obliged to be cunning and make the most of a little.

With best wishes for the success of your Memorial, and your future prosperity, I am, dear Sir, your most obedient servant,

B Franklin

Once I became the architect of my life and created a life that I loved again I was happy for a while. Before long, though, I started to feel a sense of unease because it seemed that something was still missing from my journey of *Life Alchemy*. I grappled with it for a while, studying happy, fulfilled people in the process. I inquired into what gave those people meaning and what, exactly made them happy and fulfilled.

I read stories of happy, fulfilled people; I interviewed others; I was on a quest to get to the bottom of what made them tick. I remembered one of the happiest people I ever met and what he taught me. Years ago, when I was very first trying to do anything at all to get away from the conversations in my own head about the abduction, I volunteered regularly at a soup kitchen in New York City called the Bowery Mission. The Bowery Mission serves people who are down on their luck; they provide a clean set of clothes, a hot meal, a bed, and a shower for those who are looking to get back on their feet again. The Bowery Mission helps people find employment and get a second chance in life—often at a time when society isn't so keen on giving them a second chance. While serving food there one weekend, I met a wonderful man there by the name of Brother Thomas. Brother Thomas had at one point been a recipient of the services the Bowery Mission provides; he'd made a success of himself and had come back to the Mission to provide what he could for those going through what he had previously dealt with. In addition to a contagiously warm spirit, Brother Thomas had a quote that has never left my mind, "Each One, Help One."

"What if it were really that simple?" I wondered. "What if each one of us simply had to reach out and help another one?"

Brother Thomas's journey meant all the more to him because now he could help others make the same resurrection with their lives.

"Each One, Help One." Words to live by.

Just like in the case of Brother Thomas, I found that without exception every truly happy and fulfilled person I came across had a life that was bigger than just themselves. They weren't constituted as a small individual; they saw themselves as the whole; they saw their happiness and fulfillment linked to the happiness and fulfillment of all other people. They lived for others, they contributed to others, they had something to give to others and they gave it to them lovingly. Some of these people had fortunes to give, some of them didn't have two pennies to rub together, but they all shared a generosity of spirit and an unquenchable desire to be of service.

Studying those people I realized that my own triumph in transmuting my life and my circumstances meant nothing if I didn't give it away. Don't get me wrong; it was great for me, and it was nice for my friends and family who no longer had to be worried about me and/or be impacted by my wound, but what difference did my struggle make if I didn't share the journey in such a way that other people were empowered in dealing with their own struggles?

So I got training in how to "formally" give my triumph away; I became educated in coaching and leading seminars so that I could impact the largest number of people possible.

Let's face it; one thing we all share as human beings is having crappy circumstances that we wished hadn't happened. Like it or not, bad things do happen to good people, and there's nothing we can do about that. What we *can* do is alter how we react to those things that happen. I set out on a mission to give away my story to help people deal with the things that happen that they didn't want. I figured I'd never run out of people to talk to!

Now it was crystal clear that the final step of *the Life Alchemy Method* is for a person to give away the triumph of their transmutation so that it benefits others. To have what you learned integrate into your life and be real for you, you have to give it away so that it positively impacts

148

other people. Then and only then will your journey of *Life Alchemy* be complete.

I have a confession to make: I struggled with this step. Although I'd long decided to use the transmutation I'd personally experienced in my life to make a difference with other people who were dealing with breaking free of the grip of the circumstances in their own lives, I wasn't always public about my own situation. Sure, having been abducted was *the whole reason* why I'd gone on a journey of self discovery and healing all those years ago; furthermore, it was *the reason* why I'd become a seminar leader and coach, so I could pass on the gift to others. Even so, I still never spoke about my own *Defining Incident* until decades after the event happened.

One autumn evening I was leading a seminar with hundreds of people in the room. I was engaged in an interaction with a woman who was up at the front of the room at the microphone. The woman had just openly shared with all of us that she was dealing with a bitter and painful divorce; her ex-husband had been abusive to both her and her children. The woman insisted that she could not forgive him; she could not move on; there was no getting past the betrayal and the hurt she'd endured.

I ensured her that she could move on; I told her that she could put those circumstances in the past and create a life that she loved.

"Never," she said sternly, beginning to cry, and going back to recounting publicly her story of just how bad the physical, emotional and sexual abuse had been...and it had been *bad*.

The room started to turn; I could feel I was losing people as they were beginning to side with the woman. Who could blame them? I mean, there is no one alive who couldn't relate to this woman's pain and sense of betrayal; she'd felt deeply wounded, and rightfully so.

I realized what I had to do; I had to share my story and illustrate that it *was* possible to move beyond *Defining Incidents* that are unspeakable. Sure, I could take a stand for the fact that I know she could put her divorce and the abuse behind her, but unless I could share something that was equally horrible that I'd transmuted, it was all just hypothetical for her and everyone in the room.

For years, I didn't ever open my mouth about the abduction to anyone. Literally, I told no one in the world until I got a therapist, and then I only told her. This was the first time I ever considered sharing my story aloud outside of therapy; and certainly the first time I'd ever considered sharing it publicly.

Remember how I mentioned earlier that I believe that each of us gets stuck developmentally at the age we were when we had any of our various *Defining Incidents*? I believe that I was still stuck back at my nineteenth birthday in this area. At the time, I wouldn't tell anyone that it happened, not Lizzie, not my mom or dad, not my family…no one, because I felt embarrassed that it happened to me. I felt deep down that it was my fault that it occurred; I felt that it made me unclean and unworthy and dirty. I also felt at the time that if I went there and experienced it again by telling anyone that I'd never be able to put myself back together again. I lived by compartmentalizing my life and pretending that it never happened.

This response was understandable and even appropriate for a nineteen-year-old; it was no longer appropriate given the fact that I was a full-grown woman who had transmuted that *Defining Incident* for myself, and for thousands of others as a result.

So I opened my mouth.

As the woman stood at the microphone, crying, people were getting restless in the room. Several people were getting up out of their seats and milling around at the back of the room, and a couple of people even walked out. Finally, I let it out. I shared openly, honestly and completely about what happened to me when I was nineteen and the fact that I'd never shared it before. You could have heard a pin drop.

Not long afterward I was interviewed for a documentary film called *Discover The Gift*, which featured leaders, speakers and authors such as Jack Canfield, Mark Victor Hansen, Michael Beckwith and the Dalai Lama. The director of the film called me in initially because he'd been in several seminars that I'd led and he knew he could count on me to tell it to him straight. He showed me a rough cut of the film and asked me my thoughts. I told him that the film was beautifully shot; it had an amazing cast, and it had a heartfelt message that I thought was precisely what the world needed to hear. I candidly told him that the film was entitled *Discover The Gift*, not *"Talk About The Gifts We Already Have"* so I'd hoped that he'd have stories of people who had taken hideous junk and turned that into a gift. "That," I told him, "I'd line up to see."

He asked me if I was free to shoot the next day. I made myself available.

We arrived at a beautiful location in Malibu and he and his crew turned the camera on me.

I hesitated for a moment as all of those thoughts and feelings of the nineteen-year-old inside of me welled up for a moment. "Should I say it? There's no turning back if I do; once it's on film, it'll be out of my hands, and it'll be out there *forever*."

I quelled the fears of the nineteen-year-old, and I smiled. "What else am I going to do with my life?" I said to myself; then I breathed deeply and told my tale.

When the movie came out, I invited my mom to come to Los Angeles for the premiere; I first had to let her know my story so it wouldn't come as a shock to her once she saw it on the big screen.

Recently, as I was wrapping up the manuscript for this book, I sent out an email to my close friends and family asking them to vote on the best subtitle for the book. I popped off a quick email that read, "The book is the story of how I turned the abduction and rape into a blessing, and then a step-by-step process for others to do the same in their life with any less-than-desirable circumstances they may have. My premise is: let's face it; what it is to be human is to have stuff happen which we wish hadn't. This is a guide on how to use everything life has handed you to catapult yourself into the life of your dreams."

The next morning I got a call from my dad before dawn; he woke me up.

"What are you talking about?" He asked.

I asked him the same question right back.

He told me he sat down to read his emails with his morning coffee, and he read mine; he knew nothing about any abduction or rape, so he called me to find out why.

I was mortified; I couldn't believe he didn't know. It was no surprise; I'd not spoken about it initially for years; he wasn't in my seminars, and when I invited him and my step mom to fly out for the screening of *Discover the Gift* they had to cancel their trip at the last moment, so I forgot to have the conversation with him.

I've had four subsequent conversations with him on the topic; he's been incredibly generous and gracious about it.

"I can kinda see why you didn't tell me when it happened," he said. "It's because of that Sir Galahad thing dads do."

I asked him to explain what he meant. He told me that when their kids get hurt—especially their little girls—what most dads want to do is go out there and kill the bastards.

"That probably wasn't what you needed at the time. You probably just needed to be heard or held. I'm a lot better at that now in my old age," he said.

I love my dad so much it hurts. I promised him that I would never again keep from him the important things in my life—good or bad. That I'm able to make that promise is a function of having "grown up" myself in that area. I'm no longer a nineteen-year-old in the body of a woman.

If you want mastery in anything, the accepted wisdom is you need to teach that thing; in other words, you need to give it away. So naturally, the fifth and final tenet is *You Only Get to Keep What You Give Away*. This is where the rubber really meets the road; this is where you have to take out into the world all that you've been trying on and experimenting. If you want to integrate this whole new way of living and make it part of you, then you need to start giving it away.

As you give away what you're learning, the tenets become ingrained in your thinking, and so you begin to "default" to them naturally, rather than automatically sinking back into the habits of the well-worn neural pathways that have had you stuck in the mire of victimhood or survivor status. The process of "giving it away" forces you to use language in a new way (both internally as thinking, and externally as speaking) and that new use of thinking and speaking will allow you to begin to groove new neural pathways that are consistent with the new life you're committed to living.

In the meantime, here are two additional case studies to illustrate the fifth and final tenet in a new way.

Chapter Twenty

Case Study: Sarah

S arah is a singer who came to me to work on taking her career to the next level. She mostly did session-musician work, gigs for hire, and the occasional wedding. She is very talented and wanted to record an album to shop around in hopes of getting a recording contract. Sarah wanted to both unleash her creativity and increase her productivity.

She had a blossoming singing career in her 20's, but she had given it up when she and her husband learned she was pregnant. Making music faded completely from her life of being a wife and mom to two. Now that the kids were getting older and both in school, Sarah was ready to return to her passion.

In our first several sessions we dealt with her career alone. I gave her assignments, and she fulfilled them with excitement and vigor. Sarah was making headway and had already written a new song, which was something she had not done in years.

Our fourth session took a turn. One of Sarah's daughters has been being regularly picked-on by some bigger girls at school, and the issue drove up something unresolved for Sarah.

As the session began, Sarah apologized; she said she knew that she told me we were going to work on her music career, but since this had been happening to her daughter she had no interest in discussing her music career at all. That's fine; as human beings, we can't separate the different areas of our life one from another…despite the fact that we say things like, "In my personal life," and "In my love life," all the time. If what was there for Sarah to discuss was what her daughter's upset brought up, that's what there was for her to discuss.

"This is exactly the kind of thing I tried to protect them from," Sarah said, looking away. "I've done everything in my power to make sure no one hurts them."

She broke down and cried.

"My daughter is hurting so much and I don't know what to do about it. It seems there's nothing I can say or do to make her feel better. I swore this would never happen."

I asked her what she meant.

Sarah revealed that as a young girl she had been sexually molested by her stepfather over a period of four years. Sarah moved out of her home as a young teenager, completed her GED and moved across the country.

"It had always been there at the back of my mind haunting me, but one day I decided just to let it all go," Sarah said. "The day I decided to let it go was the day I learned I was pregnant. I realized I was unwilling to pass along any of my past to my children. I never speak of it; no one else but my husband knows that it happened; no one ever will."

We discussed the molestation for the rest of the session; Sarah confided in me that it felt good to finally discuss the event; she'd never done that before with anyone but her husband and even then only in the most basic of ways. As an only child, there was no automatic person with whom Sarah would have spoken about the event. Her stepfather had since left her mother; she'd never seen him again, and her mother had then passed away. When Sarah said she never spoke about the molestation, she literally meant she *never spoke about the molestation*.

It's clear that Sarah is a healthy, well-adjusted person. She is a wonderful mother, a great wife, and a gracious, generous friend. Her life works. There's no question to any of that. What I did wonder, however, is what would happen if Sarah could be public about the molestation that had happened in her past. The week following our conversation discussing it was revolutionary for Sarah; she contacted me four times saying that she felt alive and enthused in a way she could never remember before having felt.

I asserted to her that it's because she was able to speak about the event. I asked her what might be possible if she were able to be public about the molestation. To be clear, I am in no way suggesting that Sarah start telling everyone about the event. I am certainly not advising her to start "trauma sharing" to anyone who will listen. I am also not implying that she backslide into being a survivor or that she wear the molestation as a so-called badge of honor.

What I am suggesting, however, is that she might be able to contribute it to others here and there. The very act of giving away what she had learned by enduring the horror of the event could resolve it for her in a way that simply "not speaking about it again" never could.

Sarah disagreed; she was unwilling to speak with anyone about it on any occasion. Whether she felt that she wasn't strong enough to bear bringing the event back into the present moment by speaking about it, or whether she just felt it was best to leave well enough alone, I don't know;

what I do know is that she chose to never speak about the molestation again. I've got no judgment about that; Sarah did what she felt was best for her and that is her prerogative and her God-given right.

All I know is that it is tough to be a teenager, and when Sarah's kids reach that age, they might really be able to relate to her experience of having been completely alone in the world. That is, after all, a common human experience, particularly when a person is a teenager. Sexual molestation is unlikely something that Sarah's kids would ever endure, at least not within their own home, but what is certain is that they will experience things that will be deeply upsetting. That's a part of being alive. When a person like Sarah can share the unfavorable circumstances that she's successfully dealt with, overcome, and put in the past, that same victory becomes possible for anyone who listens to the story.

As a postscript, I'm happy to announce that Sarah is now in the recording studio recording an album of her original songs.

Chapter Twenty-One

Case Study: Helen

Helen's is a story of someone who was confronted with a situation that she wouldn't have chosen for herself. The situation with which she was faced could have been a tragedy for her, and has, in fact been a tragedy for many others, but in this story the woman chose to turn her situation into a blessing. She used what life had given her to perform *Life Alchemy.*

Helen came to me to work on her career. She felt she'd hit a plateau and wasn't going anywhere, and she knew if she continued on the same path she'd be setting herself up for disaster.

Once a rising hotshot chef, Helen decided to leave the high-stress world of the kitchen to consult restaurant owners and occasionally open, run, and manage restaurants as well. The restaurant business that had once enlivened her now imprisoned her; she'd made herself indispensable to her clients, and they were unwilling to work with anyone else. Helen worked long hours, including nights and weekends;

she had no time off, and she was begrudging her job. She dreamed of expanding her business and taking on employees, but none of her clients wanted to work with her staff; they only wanted Helen.

On top of all of that, Helen had an unfulfilled dream she was doing nothing about. Once, long ago Helen got the chance to speak publicly during a press event for a celebrity-chef restaurant she was opening and the idea of one day having a public speaking career never left her. Problem was, Helen had no self-confidence in speaking with groups. One-on-one with her clients or staff she was fine, but she was afraid of speaking with more than one person at a time.

Helen and I had been working together for nearly a month when she was diagnosed with stage-three breast cancer.

She went in for a routine mammogram, and got the news; they said they'd detected a slight abnormality. Helen's doctor insisted that there was a less than 1% chance that the abnormality they detected was cancer, and they said she could simply wait until her next mammogram to see if it developed into anything.

Helen said no; she insisted that they biopsy the breast. She later told me that usually she didn't like to look too far into things for fear of what she'd find, but this was different. She said that because of the work the two of us had been doing by "digging around" in her past by delving into her *Defining Incidents*, she felt she had the confidence to dig around with regard to her health.

Helen's doctors biopsied the breast and came back with results: she not only had breast cancer, but advanced, aggressive breast cancer.

Helen says that there was a split second after she was diagnosed where she thought, "Why me?" and cursed her fate. She caught herself in the act, walked to the mirror and calmly spoke to herself.

Helen picked up the phone and called me. We spoke and dismantled the *Defining Incident* as it was occurring, so that rather than creating new coping mechanisms, Helen was powerfully related to reality, and she had her full faculties available to her. When she had power again, we ended the call.

She looked back in the mirror, saying, "Why not me?" to her reflection.

She refused to leave the mirror, she later said, until she had sorted herself out.

"Sorting myself out," Helen later recounted, "meant that I resolved for myself that I would not allow myself to indulge in self pity. I spoke a solemn vow into the mirror, as I looked deep into my eyes, that I would embrace what was happening. I decided I was not going to merely survive it, tolerate it, or accept it; I was going to embrace it.

Helen then dialed her doctor.

"Alright," she told him. "Let's get in there, and let's take them both."

Her doctor told her she didn't need a double mastectomy; the cancer was only in one breast. Helen didn't want to deal with a mastectomy a second time, should the cancer ever come back, so she decided to deal with the cancer proactively.

In virtually every instance," Helen later told, "There was a moment where my mind could have gone either way. There was always a split-second choice to be made where I could have been bitter and angry and resentful, or I could have been upbeat about the whole thing. I kept choosing the high road. I refused to create any more coping mechanisms this time. It was hard at first, but each time I chose the high road it got easier to choose it. Thank God we'd already been doing the coaching work together; it made life so much easier."

"Let's do this thing!" Helen said to her surgeon. "I've always been too flat-chested as it is. It's not every day a girl gets a chance to start over and re-design her looks, you know."

Helen had the double mastectomy. Soon after she began chemotherapy and radiation.

It was while sitting in chemotherapy one morning that I asked Helen if she was willing to engage in a coaching conversation with me about the cancer.

"That's why I called you here!" Helen joked. "I bet it's the first time you've ever coached someone while they're actually undergoing chemotherapy."

She was right.

I knew that for Helen to truly walk free, she was going to eventually have to be willing to take responsibility for the creation of the cancer. Again, remember that I am not talking about blame or "being guilty for" or any other negative, disempowering interpretation. I'm talking about being willing to claim that you are at the font or wellspring of all that comes into your human experience.

I broached the subject with Helen. She sat in silence. A few minutes later she said, "It was in the instant that you asked me that question that I had an epiphany. I was sitting in silence thinking about my life and how I got to this place."

And then she smiled. She smiled and started a silent laugh that made her body shake with laughter. Soon tears streamed down the sides of her face.

"I've been praying," she began, "for a vacation. I've been unwilling to take one...I've been unwilling to do that because I've been afraid that if I do, all of my clients will find someone to replace me. They'll realize in my absence that they don't really need me; that they can do what I do better than I'm doing it; that I'm not necessary. So I never rest. Never. I work seven days a week, and I suffer. Silently, as I lay my head down each night, though, I pray that I'll find a way to take time off, to just get a break."

She hung her head for a millisecond, then picked her head back up and looked me square in the eye.

"I did it; didn't I? I sure got what I wanted and then some."

I nodded.

Helen just stared at me in the eye and nodded back. "Wow," was all she could say.

A while later, I left. Helen called me that evening and shared with me what happened after I left. Helen likened her experience to the peeling back of the proverbial onion. Layer after layer was taken away until she got down to something of substance.

"I peeled away my overwhelming need to get a break that had driven me to this point. Then I peeled away my breasts, and my hair, and my eyebrows. I peeled away my obsession with my job, and my social life, and my friends. I peeled away my concerns about my weight, and my appearance, and all my insecurities. All that peeling back left me with an empty space. I sat in the emptiness that day in chemotherapy. I didn't fight the emptiness; I didn't attempt to fill it up, and I didn't resist it. I just allowed it to be."

In that empty space, Helen said, she discovered a profound relationship to who she is and what is essential in life.

"It felt like nirvana," Helen said. "Or at least what I imagine people mean when they say nirvana."
In that space of being fully present and related to reality, Helen said she came alive.

"Once I tasted that experience, I knew life would never be the same," she said. "I realized that what really matters is very simple. We mistakenly put all the importance on the things that have no importance or relevance or impact. I kept fighting the situations that life handed me. All my life I'd been doing that, I'd been competing with myself, with others, or with imaginary ideals. I was unwilling to let go of control; I was unwilling to relax or take any time off. I was always fighting life until that very moment when I realized I could embrace what life handed me."

She kept coming in for chemotherapy and radiation.

"Don't get me wrong," Helen said, "the treatment was awful. It was horrible. But at the same time it was the catalyst that had me see what really matters in life. It was the catalyst that had me see that we are always creating our lives…just most of the time we're not aware that we're doing it. I realized if I could create cancer; I could create absolutely anything I set my mind to. That made this whole experience a very good thing!" People wondered why she was always in such a good mood while she was in treatment.

"Some people get a diagnosis," Helen said, "whether it's cancer, pre-cancer or a misdiagnosis—maybe it's even a diagnosis in the non-literal sense of the word—and they immediately think it's a death sentence. They just give up. They lie down and die. I realized that could be me. I was unwilling to have it go that way."

When it was time to rebuild her breasts, Helen was upbeat about that, too. "I'm going to be like Barbie by the time I get through," she joked.

Her oncologist continued to be pleased and surprised by her attitude. He was so pleased and surprised that he asked Helen if she would be willing to go around the oncology ward with him and speak with some of his other patients in the hopes that some of Helen's optimism would wear off on them. Helen agreed.

The other patients loved her. Helen is candid and down to earth; she's a "salt of the earth" kind of person to whom the other patients naturally related. In her own words, Helen says, "I'm just a farm girl from Des Moines. People relate to me."

Her matter-of-fact relationship to the cancer coupled with her refusal to be brought down was contagious. Helen's oncologist and the rest of the cancer department at UCLA Medical Center were so inspired by how she related to her own bout with cancer, that they began asking Helen to come speak to their patients each time she was getting chemotherapy or radiation.

She agreed every time. Helen spoke with those newly diagnosed with cancer, patients going through radiation, those deliberating getting chemotherapy, and those confronting a lumpectomy or a mastectomy.

The irony was this: before cancer, Helen had fantasized about some day being a public speaker of some kind. Being a public speaker was an unlikely eventuality for her, though because she was previously so shy and reserved around those she didn't know well.

When Helen was asked to speak to patients in the cancer ward, she did it because, "These people could use my help." Her own concerns of being shy or nervous to speak in front of others never came into the equation; she wasn't doing this for herself; she was doing it for them.

Before long, Helen's doctor started calling her in to speak with other patients when she wasn't there for treatment. Other oncologists did as well. A non-profit group that services the hospital learned of the difference Helen was making with the patients and asked her to speak to the various groups for which they provide programs. She agreed.

"Finally my hair started to grow back," Helen recounted. "Eventually, the typical worries of life started to re-emerge: I was back to obsessing about work, nit-picking about my weight, and obsessing about relationships."

Helen realized that the game in life from that point forward would be to stay in touch with that "nirvana moment" and to put her focus on that which matters.

It's three years since Helen was diagnosed. She is cancer-free. She now works for the non-profit; she's become a public speaker for them, and she designs programs for the public on their behalf.

Helen will tell anybody who ever asks that the cancer was the best thing that ever happened in her entire life.

People are diagnosed with cancer every day; that's nothing special. Helen's relationship to the cancer, however, is truly extraordinary. She's a prime example of a person who achieved *Life Alchemy*.

We can't control the things that happen to us.

Like in the case of Helen, we can't control what diseases we get. Sure you can eat healthily and be a virtual poster child for clean living, but one could argue the case that Helen was just that. She was a triathlete who worked out regularly, ate organic food and avoided chemicals, plastics, and processed food. How could cancer possibly happen to her? She was only in her 30's.

The point is we can't control a darn thing that happens, but if we can control how we respond to what happens, then we can have the say so in how life goes from that point forward. Then we've really got something; we've got our hands on the wheel, and we can actually control that which really matters most.

All of us aren't handed a situation such as aggressive cancer in the way Helen was; a life-and-death proposition like that can cause a person to make a 180-degree change in an instant. With most of us there's no "need" to change; we just live in silent despair coupled with flickers of hope and wish that things would be different.

We resign ourselves to the fact that "that's just the way life is," or "that's just the way the world is," or "that's just the way I am." We attempt to assure ourselves and anyone else that will listen that it will be different "someday."

We never consider for a moment that our entire reality is a constructed reality, and that if we created what we have currently, then we could re-create it to be anything we choose. We don't look to ourselves as the source of things being the way they are.

Because of the fact we aren't all handed life-and-death situations like Helen's to turn our lives around is the reason I created this step-by-step, *Life Alchemy Method*. Rather than waiting until circumstances are grave and you are confronted with a life-or-death prospect, you can transmute the lead in your life into gold now, on demand.

Chapter Twenty-Two

Postscript

None of us can control the circumstances that happen to us. Circumstances will show up; situations will befall us; things we wish wouldn't happen, will happen. No matter what we may hope to the contrary, there's no control over any of that. As much as I'd like to believe life goes in some other way, sometimes bad stuff happens to good people. It's just a fact of life. The one thing that we do have control over, however, is our response. We can control how we contextualize what happens, what we call what happens and whether we name what happens a blessing or a curse.

How do you know what to "*use*"?

Start with what you've got in front of you.

Want to know what is "meant to be"?

Consider that what is meant to be: is.

Want to be on your perfect path? Want to know you're living God's will? *Then keep going forward, take everything life hands you exactly the way it is and exactly the way it isn't and use it in the day-to-day living of your life.*

Now, you could say, "I'm using it!" when someone cuts you off in traffic, and you flip them off or chase them down and give them a piece of your mind. Like, "Hey, life gave me a jerk, and I "used it" by responding accordingly!" No. *How* you use it is as essential as *that* you use it. How you use it has always got to be in alignment with your purpose and your highest vision for your life.

Earlier in the book I mentioned to you that none of what I was about to tell you was the truth; it was just a possible way of looking at things that I hoped would give you both closure and power. And while that was certainly correct up until this point, now I am going to tell you something that *is true*: **you are extraordinary**.

You've not only dealt with a lot in your life, but you're the kind of person who would take a journey like this book provides to learn how to move past the things with which you've dealt. Not everyone is willing to do that; look around if you don't believe me. The news is overflowing with stories of individuals who have lashed out and retaliated for the hand they were dealt. It's rare, comparatively speaking; that a person would voluntarily choose to take responsibility for all that's happened in their lives, transmute it into gold, and to pay the lesson that they've learned forward.

You are one of the few; you are one of the dignified; you are one of the elite; you get to breathe the rarified air at the mountaintop because you've chosen the high road. You are a champion, and it is my honor to have shared this part of your journey with you.

I would love the opportunity to continue this journey with you, and I've created two ways for you to do that. To assist you in this process, I have created both the Use It Video Training Series—which is filled with step-by-step exercises and processes designed to transform your life—as well as the live Use It Seminar—so that you can meet and network with other like-minded individuals as well as having the opportunity to work with me one-on-one. Both of these opportunities are designed to help you achieve Life Alchemy. To learn more, visit:

www.CherylHunter.com/training

I leave you with one final charge: don't wait until you have figured something out to be the biggest, fullest expression of yourself; you're ready now. Trust me; you're ready. The world wants and needs what you have to give; we're waiting for you. Get yourself into the world; get out there with people; give away your gifts; and *live*. It's time to become the fullest expression of your awesome self again. Go.

:

About the Author

Cheryl Hunter is an author, speaker and high-performance coach who has coached and led personal development seminars for over 86,000 people since 1995. She teaches courses of her own design in universities, coaches executives in global corporations and works one-on-one with individuals to help them live happier, more productive and fulfilling lives. A frequent on-camera host, Cheryl is currently featured as the coach in an AOL/Huffington Post series. In addition to being an author, Cheryl is a contributing writer to several national publications. Cheryl became a coach as a result of her own life path; she moved overseas as a teenager to become a fashion model and was abducted, beaten, and left for dead. Her journey back gave her a strong desire to contribute to others and give away what she had learned. She shares her triumphant story in her TEDx talk: Wabi-Sabi: The Magnificence Of Imperfection.

Made in the USA
Charleston, SC
07 October 2012